The Zen of
Cat Walking

The Zen of Cat Walking

LEASH TRAIN YOUR CAT AND UNLEASH YOUR MIND

CLIFFORD BROOKS

Skyhorse Publishing

All inquiries should be addressed to Skyhorse Publishing, 307 West 36th Street, 11th Floor, New York, NY 10018.

Skyhorse Publishing books may be purchased in bulk at special discounts for sales promotion, corporate gifts, fund-raising, or educational purposes. Special editions can also be created to specifications. For details, contact the Special Sales Department, Skyhorse Publishing, 307 West 36th Street, 11th Floor, New York, NY 10018 or info@skyhorsepublishing.com.

Skyhorse® and Skyhorse Publishing® are registered trademarks of Skyhorse Publishing, Inc.®, a Delaware corporation.

Visit our website at www.skyhorsepublishing.com.

10 9 8 7 6 5 4 3 2 1

Library of Congress Cataloging-in-Publication Data
Names: Brooks, Clifford, 1959- author.
Title: The zen of cat walking : leash train your cat and unleash your mind / Clifford Brooks.
Description: New York, New York : Skyhorse Publishing, [2018] | Includes bibliographical references and index.
Identifiers: LCCN 2017046002 (print) | LCCN 2017058932 (ebook) | ISBN 9781510726307 (E-book) | ISBN 9781510726291 (hardcover : alk. paper) | ISBN 9781510726307 (ebook)
Subjects: LCSH: Cats—Training.
Classification: LCC SF446.6 (ebook) | LCC SF446.6 .B765 2018 (print) | DDC 636.8/0835—dc23
LC record available at https://lccn.loc.gov/2017046002

Cover design by Mona Lin
Cover illustration by Stephanie Medeiros

Hardcover ISBN: 978-1-5107-2629-1
eBook ISBN: 978-1-5107-2630-7

Printed in China

DEDICATION

To Greg Brandenburgh. Thank you for providing a strong and loving push along the path to enlightenment.
    I love you like a dead relative.

SPECIAL THANKS

To the many cats who showed me that one's worth is the sum of one's deeds, and to the cat walkers who shared their remarkable stories with me. We are one big family.

TABLE OF CONTENTS

MEDITATIONS

INTRODUCTION

"I have lived with several Zen masters—all of them cats."
—*Eckhart Tolle,* The Power of Now: A Guide to
Spiritual Enlightenment

Common wisdom insists that cats are not dogs and shouldn't be asked to walk on a leash. If you're foolish enough to attempt it, well-meaning friends and family members may try to set you straight. They'll tell you that cats are too independent and dignified to walk on a leash. Some of them will shake their heads and laugh. Others will share stories of their own feline failures. Most of them will wonder why you would even try such a thing.

But no one knows your cat like you do. If you're like me, you see your cat sitting in the window, separated from the natural world by a thin pane of glass, and you feel a pang of regret. You know he longs to be a part of that world, to feel the wind and the sun on his coat, to stalk birds and squirrels, to eat grass, and to become a participant instead of just an observer. And you think, maybe, just maybe, you have one of those rare cats who don't bow to common wisdom, a cat who has never been told he can't walk on a leash.

The odds aren't good, but then you look over at your cat and he's still in the window, laser-focused and chattering away at a blue jay in the yard, and you decide right then and there that you'll never know if your cat is that rare individual unless you try.

The last hurdle may be your self-esteem. Because cat walking is still on the societal fringe, you may fear how your efforts will be judged by your neighbors. If successful, you may be branded the crazy cat person in the neighborhood. Of course, there's also the possibility that your cat won't take to the leash, and you'll fail. Then, the neighbors may decide you're not the crazy cat person, you're just plain crazy.

And that's where it ends for many. Fortunately, there are a number of people who decide that making this happen is more important than what the neighbors might think. Still, there's a lot of baggage to unpack before going out and buying a harness and leash for your cat. But even then, as you pass the extensive row of dog-walking para-phernalia to find only one or two options for cats, doubt rears its ugly head again. So, it's no wonder that so many people give up when their cat doesn't immediately accept the harness. After being buckled in, many cats refuse to budge, or worse, they have a violent reaction and begin jumping and flipping about like a fish out of water. A portion of the remaining potential walkers stop right there, before even setting foot outdoors.

This leaves a small group of dedicated people; the lucky ones whose cat accepts the harness outright and those who realize that this is a really big deal for their cat and decide to give their cat the time he needs to adjust. This book was written for those people. If you're willing to invest in your cat, you could end up proudly wearing the crazy cat person mantle and significantly enriching your cat's life in the process.

This book also serves as a Zen meditation primer. The idea came to me after I'd titled the book. Initially, the connection to Zen was limited. My original intent was to simply emphasize the fact that to be successful at cat walking, you would need to exercise patience, calm, and perspective. In my own life, these qualities were greatly enhanced by my exploration and practice of Zen and other forms of meditation.

Meditation is both the easiest and the hardest thing I've ever done. Learning what to do is deceptively simple, as there's very little to it. It's sitting and breathing, or sitting and reciting a mantra, or, in the case of guided meditation, it's about refocusing your mind on the images and sounds that the guide provides. While each form of meditation differs in the fine details and underlying philosophy, they all rely on quieting and deactivating the random thoughts by redirecting your attention elsewhere. Once you've reduced the mental chaos to a manageable level, you can dive down beneath it to a calm place that enables introspection and leads to enlightenment.

Conceptually easy, but when you sit down to meditate, things get difficult fast. I found keeping focused on my breath or maintaining a mantra the most difficult thing I've ever attempted. The thoughts return unbidden and it's often difficult to realize the focus shift has occurred until you've gone on for breathless minutes. It's no wonder it's so difficult; your mind has been in control all your life, so relinquishing some of that control doesn't come easily. It requires practice. The more you practice, the better you will get, but I can't stress this enough: this is not about the destination, there is no endpoint, and the success will feel very uneven in the early stages.

The benefits of meditation are well-documented and numerous. Inner calm and reduced stress have numerous health benefits. Your relationships will benefit as you gain the ability to see things more clearly and less emotionally. And you may experience changes, personal changes, that you never expected.

I began my meditation journey in response to a severe TMJ problem. TMJ is a condition that can cause extreme pain, headaches, and temporary locking of the jaw. The temporomandibular joint is the point where your jaw connects to the temporal bones of your skull. TMJ is an inflammation of the joint caused by teeth grinding and stress. At its worst, it can be completely debilitating. So far there really isn't a cure; flare-ups are most commonly treated with muscle relaxants, painkillers, splints, and hot and cold compresses. None of these treatments worked for me, and a bad flare-up would have me bedridden, writhing in pain, for a couple of weeks.

During one such flare-up, I was given everything from codeine to Valium, but nothing worked. At all. The effect was the same as if I'd taken a Life Saver, though not nearly as pleasant. I assumed that I had a weird metabolism that kept me from feeling the effects of drugs. That's what I believed at the time.

In desperation, I tried meditation.

In the early days, I didn't feel any change. I was going through the motions, meditating four or five days a week, but it felt like I was struggling with the discursive thoughts that peppered my consciousness without realizing any real benefits.

Except, I was.

I had been meditating for about six months when I found myself in a rooftop restaurant bar, sharing a glass of wine and freshly grilled shish kebabs with a friend. It was a beautiful San Francisco evening in the Mission District, and on my way to the restroom, I walked to the roof's edge to look down at the bustle of activity on the street below.

As I turned away from the edge, I felt a strange, light feeling. It was disconcerting at first, but when I returned to our table, I told my friend:

"I think I just felt the effects of alcohol for the first time."

He smiled, and in his gentle way left the door open for me to talk about it. Which I did. It probably sounded silly, but it was a huge moment for me.

To say it was on my mind a lot that week is an understatement. Could the meditation be working? Was this a corollary effect? And as I ruminated, I realized I hadn't had a flare-up since I'd begun meditating and the clicking in my jaw was nearly gone.

And then I began to dream again, or at least, I remembered them. Something I hadn't done since childhood.

Nobody told me that meditation would impact me so profoundly. But it did. I felt like I'd been released from a self-imposed prison. One I'd built up since childhood and mortared with the best stuff I could find to protect myself from the world. It was scary and freeing and a little uncomfortable.

Where would this take me, I wondered, and still wonder.

Like cat walking, learning to meditate takes time. How much time? This too is like cat walking as neither endeavor has an end-point. Meditation is a practice. It benefits the sitter in ways that are not immediately apparent and even on those days when the meditation "doesn't go well," you're still making progress below the surface.

This book discusses Zen, but all meditation is similar and if you practice, or would like to practice, an alternative, feel free. My own meditation practice is neither fish nor fowl; I've taken the bits that work for me from various disciplines and created my own practice out of it. I hope, after reading this book, you feel comfortable enough to do the same with both your meditation and cat-walking practice.

About This Book

The Zen of Cat Walking includes easy-to-follow instructions on teaching your cat to walk on a leash, ruminations on cat behavior, and notes on Zen meditation. The latter has been advocating a level of calm and appreciation that's sure to benefit both you and your cat as you embark on sympathetic journeys. Using step-by-step cat-training instructions, notes on Zen meditation, and insightful profiles of successful cat walkers, you will learn how cat walking can have a healthy impact on your life and the life of your feline friend.

Cat walking, like Zen meditation, is a practice and not a destination. Don't expect stair-step-like results; a great walk or meditation can be followed by what you consider a disaster the next time out. Don't fret. This is how it works, and even though you come away disappointed, you and your cat have both grown. Both meditation and cat walking require a bit of trust. You need to believe that in time you'll turn a corner and begin to realize the benefits of your practices.

THE TRUTH ABOUT CATS AND DOGS

My childhood cat, a black-and-white tuxedo, was an indoor-outdoor cat. We lived in a Victorian in a quiet Midwestern town on a tree-lined street free from excessive traffic. He had the run of the house, the yard, and the world across the garden wall. He was a great cat, an explorer, and even though I was the only cat person in the house when he arrived, as cats are wont to do, he endeared himself to the entire family.

He was good about returning home, but like most normal unfixed toms, he would sometimes disappear for days at a time. When he'd return, nonplussed by our attentions, he would rejoin his normal routine until the need hit him again to wander.

We loved that cat. At the time, our naive disregard for his welfare was typical in the community. Most of the cats in town were indoor-outdoor cats, like ours. Few spayed or neutered their cats and even fewer kept them trapped inside all day. And whenever the town toyed with extending its leash laws to include cats, owners extended their claws in defense of their cat's independent nature, opining that it wasn't natural to put a cat on a leash. They were meant to be free, after all.

And so it was.

But as their numbers ballooned and the number of cats in homes began to rival, and then surpass, the number of dogs, people began to look closer at the welfare of cats as well as their impact on the local wildlife populations.

Nearly all responsible people have their cats fixed by six months. Most responsible cat owners keep their cats indoors, but they sense something is missing. Some of us purchase cat trees and toys and gadgets to try to simulate the natural world for them. Others take things a step further and install climbing shelves and create cat super highways so their cats can exercise their need to climb. And those with the means and the desire close in patios and porches or create freestanding or attached catios to give their cats a safe taste of the outdoors.

Is this enough?

Not really. The problem with simulations is that they lack the element of surprise. They may trigger a response, even a heightened response, but even the most adept play toy is not a bird. Or a lizard. Or a squirrel. Except for the large yard with a cat fence installed, these well-meaning solutions help alleviate boredom and should be maintained even after you've trained your cat to walk on a leash. As good as they are, they stop short of providing cats with the stimulation they need to fully feel like part of the natural world. Once playtime is over, they find themselves looking out at the world through windows and screens rather than interacting directly.

So what if, like the dog, you took your cat time outside on walks through the neighborhood? What if your cat could explore the world, interact with it, and become a part of the wider world? What then?

Are you afraid that once your cat has had a taste of the world beyond the big door he'll want more? And eventually he will eschew the couch for the flower bed and all will be lost?

That could happen, if you deny your cat regular access to the outdoors. For a while, you will want to take your cat out as frequently as possible, creating a regular routine. Unlike the dog, the reason for the outdoor trek is pure pleasure and enrichment. There are no fire hydrants to water, aerobic exercises to endure, or squirrels to tree.

Okay, your cat may engage in one or two of those things on occasion, but in most cases, it's not the reason we walk our cats. Walking a cat is a purely pleasurable activity for both you and your cat. After half an hour or so, most cats will accept the return home, knowing another trip is forthcoming, and settle in for a nice nap.

Despite what you've been told, you can teach your cat to walk on a leash. If you're lucky, your cat is already predisposed to walking, and the task will be relatively easy. For the rest of us, the journey is daunting but no less valuable. We'll need to exercise patience and empathy and love reliably and consistently if we're going to help our cat overcome his inherent fear of the leash. We'll need to look within to see if we have what it takes.

Training a cat to walk on a leash will change him in subtle and sometimes not so subtle ways. But some things won't change. Leash-trained cats still run the household, endear themselves to family members who stubbornly try to resist, and still benefit from their time with you.

During one of my post-writing meditation sessions, it hit me. Most people don't think cats can be trained because they don't need to be. Beyond getting them to use the litterbox, which comes naturally, and convincing your cat to use the scratching pole rather than the couch, most people don't consider training their cats. Some don't even believe they can learn their names.

Consider the puppy. An untrained dog can be a disaster; tearing up everything in his path, jumping, biting, and pulling so hard on his walks that his owner fears bodily harm.

Training a puppy takes time; time that people take because they must.

Ever taught a cat to "sit" on command? I can tell you, it doesn't take any longer than teaching a dog. In fact, most things don't take any longer, they're just not necessary. So now that you know the truth, teaching your cat to walk on a leash should be something you consider. It will take time, and due to the differences between cats and dogs, a bit more patience. But it can be done. It's time to rethink the way we approach cats and learning.

I'd like to end this section by stating, as concisely as I can, the five truths of cat walking. You'll notice dogs come up a lot in these descriptions. That's because no one doubts that dogs can be trained, even the stubborn ones. Keep these five truths in your mind, and even on the hardest training days you'll find the courage to go on.

The 5 Truths of Cat Walking

1. Cats are not dogs, but like dogs, they're trainable.
2. Training a dog takes time; so does training a cat.
3. Dogs must be trained, cats require very little. This is why so many cat owners give up so quickly and decide their cat is untrainable.
4. Cat fear is natural; it's a survival tactic. Cat fear is not as detrimental as you may think, and some may be helpful. Experience can rewire your cat's response to a number of fear-inducing stimuli, but it can take lots of repetition before that happens. Over time, your cat will habituate on a number of stimuli he initially finds terrifying. Cats learn.
5. Cats, even the shy/fearful ones, want to go outside.

Cat Walker: Angela Amerson

Academic Coordinator, PBS *Masterpiece* Buff, Proud Canadian, and Cat Walker

Angela Amerson was born and raised in Kingston, Ontario, Canada. She currently shares her life with her husband David and two Singapura cats. Singapuras are one of the smallest pedigree cat breeds, clocking in at 5–8 pounds when full grown. But that doesn't mean they're pushovers. What they lack in size, they make up for in moxie. Amerson's two

Singapuras, Astro and his younger sister, Gidget, are living proof that good things often come in small packages.

At the time of the interview, Gidget was at the beginning of her cat-walking journey while her older brother, Astro, had become a pro. Astro was two years old.

EARLY DAYS

Astro came from a breeder in California who flew him to Angela. When Angela took him out of his carrier at the airport, he was wearing a harness. She clipped a leash on the 4-month-old kitten and took him on his first walk, right there in the airport.

She then took him to the vet, completed his kitten shots, and got a clean bill of health before embarking on the training in earnest. When she took him outside, she would usually take a toy—something on a stick that she could dangle before him to encourage him to continue when he got distracted. She made sure that every trip outside was fun and something he looked forward to. When it was time to return home, she would say "Let's go home," and when they reached their front porch she would give him a tasty treat. So now, when she tells Astro it's time to go home, he turns and walks back home.

"Astro has brought so much joy to my life. He's brought me more joy than I could ever give him."

—*Angela Amerson*

Today, most of their walks are in their condo community. On some days, they walk more than two miles. "But not every day," Amerson explains. "When he doesn't want to walk we just hang out in the yard."

TRAINING DAYS

Astro was one of those cats that took to walking on a leash easily and early. From the first day he arrived, he began walking and hasn't stopped yet. Amerson's training was more about fine-tuning than out-and-out teaching; she used toys and other rewards to reinforce the desired behaviors.

One area that most cat walkers must deal with is their cat's fear of strangers. Even cats who don't seem to mind meeting strangers on their own turf find them overwhelming when meeting them in the great outdoors. That's not a problem for Astro.

"Astro loves people; he goes right up to them! In the summer it's a lot of fun. Neighbors will come outside to see him as we walk through the neighborhood. He loves attention, loves people, and noises make him curious. When he hears a noise, he wants to see what it is."

FOLLOWING THE LEADER

Amerson says that sometimes she leads and other times Astro takes the lead. If she has something in mind, like a trip to a butterfly garden, or when she doesn't have time for a long leisurely walk, she guides him.

"When it's time to go home or he seems to be getting tired, I ask him if he's ready to go home. On the return home he generally keeps pace with me, but if a neighbor is out, he stops and wants to socialize. If we really must get home, I pick him up and carry him past distractions."

In addition to their neighborhood walks, Amerson has taken him to the park. Fearing ticks and run-ins with total strangers and their pets, she doesn't do that often, but she loves to watch him climb big trees in the park.

TOOLS OF THE TRADE

Amerson uses a clip-on harness with Astro. When on a walk she uses a standard cat leash. When he's in the backyard and she wants to increase his range so he can chase insects and birds, she uses a much longer leash.

When asked for tips on training a cat to walk on a leash, Amerson's number one tip is patience. "Remember it's for the cat, not the owner, and if the cat doesn't want to do it, don't force it, or they'll never do it. Every time they see the harness and leash they'll run and hide. Start as early as possible; put the harness on and let the cat walk around the house with the harness and leash dragging behind it. Also, make sure you look around to see what's out there before you embark on your walk. Be safe and aware. You don't want any tragedies."

ZAZEN: THE WHY OF ZEN

"In zazen, we do not expect anything.

"Zazen is not a technique to achieve anything.

"It is much more natural.

"And yet, somehow the most natural thing is difficult to do.

"How come?

"Because we think.

"There is nothing wrong with thinking.

"Thinking is a very natural process, but we are so easily conditioned by our thinking and give too much value to it."
—*Maezumi Roshi, Zen Buddhist teacher*

With cats, fear is a survival tactic and not nearly as bad as you might think. Depending on the cat, it could take days or years for it to let go of its fears and begin to really enjoy the outdoors while on leash. To help your cat with the transition, you need to find your place of patience and inner peace and inhabit that place during your cat-walking practice. If you're anxious, impatient, or bored with the process, your negative energy will be transmitted to your cat.

You might already be there, but a lot of us aren't. If you find yourself getting impatient or spending more time reading your phone than reading your cat, stop, reassess where your head is, and work on developing a more present attitude before proceeding further. Meditation can help here.

I've been meditating for nearly ten years. My own practice is an amalgam of what I've learned from my investigations and practices. It's not Zen, it's not Transcendental Meditation (TM), and it's not rooted in religious or philosophical truths. But it contains elements of all these practices, and I couldn't have found a level of peace without them.

While Zen is a good place to start your own personal journey, any type of meditation you choose will help you relate to your cat on a deeper, richer level. My intent is to give you the tools to take that first step down the path to regular meditation.

Given that quieting the mind is about as unnatural for us as walking on a leash is for cats, embarking on this journey will, by its very nature, increase your level of patience and empathy for what your cat is going through.

Learning to meditate is a journey, and like all such journeys there may be detours and false starts along the way. That's okay. If this is something you want, eventually, you'll get there. Don't beat yourself up over it if it doesn't progress as quickly or as smoothly as you hope; meditation is both maddeningly simple and excruciatingly difficult when you first start. The practice of zazen, or seated meditation, requires that you allow yourself to fumble along the way. In the beginning, you'll spend most of your time redirecting your attention away from your thoughts and back to your breathing. That's not only all right, it's an integral part of the process. Most people feel they're failing when the mind goes on its side trips, but nothing could be further from the truth.

Allow. Redirect. Refocus.

Over time, focusing on your breath will become second nature and you will no longer spend most of your time redirecting. Until that happens, accept that fact that each time you let go of a random thought, you're exercising your meditation muscles.

So, what is Zen?

It has been said that there are as many answers as there are Zen masters. Zen is hard to describe. It's something you do. Zen is a practice where you search for enlightenment from within rather than without. The answers to your questions are within you; they come from the same place as the questions.

These answers do not come from philosophizing, rational thought, or the study of scriptures. Zen is not a religion or a philosophy. Zen is difficult, if not impossible, to define with mere words. In his book *Finding the Still Point*, the late Zen master John Daido Loori described the practice of zazen:

"To practice zazen is to study the self. In its early stages, zazen has the appearance of what is normally called meditation. But we must understand that zazen is more than just meditation. It is not mere contemplation or introspection. It is not quieting the mind or focusing the mind. Zazen is sitting Zen—one aspect of Zen. There is also walking Zen, working Zen, laughing Zen, and crying Zen. Zen is a way of using one's mind and living one's life, and doing this with other people.

No rule book has ever been written that can adequately describe Zen. You have to go very deep into yourself to find its foundation."

And while Zen may not simply be meditation, the way you "go very deep" into yourself is. You must gain greater control over your mind through the practice of meditation. You must give up overthinking and getting bogged down by the incessant chatter of the mind, making room for the truth to arise just as easily and purely as the questions.

My own meditation practice has led me to believe that regular meditation reprograms the brain. It detoxifies thought, increases focus, and allows you to tackle life's questions from a place of calm and emotional distance.

I have not experienced enlightenment.

But before enlightenment comes calm. Learning to let go, to be aware but not emotionally shackled, will put you on the road to enlightenment. In this book, I focus on the early stages of meditation; learning to let go of the discursive thoughts that distract you from your journey.

Meditation has helped me train my kittens to walk on a leash. I found that breathing, accepting, and turning off the clock were integral in being able to help them manage their fear. As a cat owner, you probably know that getting a cat to do something it doesn't want to do is futile; you must provide your cat with positive alternatives if you are to succeed in changing his behavior. When it comes to access to the outdoors, I believe even the most fearful of cats wants this.

As parents and partners and family members, we're used to telling each other what to do. It's the most expeditious route to a desired outcome, so we tend to default to this behavior even when it's not the most appropriate course of action.

It just feels right.

This doesn't often work with cats. Cats are very much in tune with their needs, so telling a cat to do something it sees no value in doesn't really work. Just like you, the cat has to find the answers for himself, the way forward from within. You are there to help your cat along the journey, not make him do what you want.

During your cat-walking practice, it's imperative that you don't let your own feelings of inadequacy, impatience, or anger at the slow pace of your cat's progress color your interactions. As soon as you feel any of these things, stop, breathe, and find that place of calm your meditation practice affords.

THE MYSTERIOUS CAT

Make no mistake about it, the cat is still a mystery. Every year researchers across the globe try to answer such fundamental questions as:

"Do cats like their owners?"

"Are cats really domesticated?"

"Do cats need us?"

"If our cats were larger, would they kill us?"

If you're a cat owner, you're probably shaking your head about now. And you should be. The answers are patently obvious to us, but for some reason, researchers approach the cat as if it were a newly discovered species, not a beloved companion animal that has lived with humans for thousands of years.

So they fashion scientific studies, answering questions we already know the answers to. The narrowness of their queries reveals more about the researchers' biases than they do about cat nature. Cat owners know one thing: most cats don't just let anyone into their world. They put up their guard, hold their secrets close, and close out all but those who they deem worthy of their trust. And trust doesn't come overnight, either. Even the sweetest, most even-tempered cat doesn't really relax in front of his owner until the owner has demonstrated good, predictable behavior over time. They may like you early on, as a playmate, and they may even expose their belly a time or two, but the kind of trust and love I'm talking about comes with time, and it's only then that a cat will let down his guard with you and let you have a peek inside the inner workings of his soul. But even then, you must look closely and perceptively if you are to see what you're being shown.

For this reason, cats don't readily bow to the scientific method. Researchers would be better off examining the domestic cat in its natural habitat: the loving home. Or simply asking us. There's little we enjoy talking about more.

Still, as cat owners, we know the answer to most of these questions first hand, but we're also the first to acknowledge that cats hold a lot of their secrets close, and we, as companions, are probably as apt to glean these truths as are all the researchers out there combined.

Many of the problems researchers face are revealed by the questions they ask. Do our cats love us? Before they can answer that, they must define love. And then they must define it in terms of a species they barely understand. So even before they begin their quest, they're hamstrung, often deciding upon measurable goals that are neither species appropriate or measurable in controlled environments. The results are often a mishmash of wishy-washy observations and extrapolations.

What about the real mysteries, the stuff that would enrich our relationships with our feline companions?

Cats are moody. Or more correctly, experience moods. They sometimes don't want to be bothered; they have other things on their minds. But when the time is right, they seek us out for cuddling, head butts, purrs, or maybe just a little time sharing the same space. Cats are individuals, and they express their affection in as many ways as there are cats. Sure, there's crossover, but it's all a matter of degree and circumstance. Your cat may be all over you one day, and strangely aloof the very next. It's all about what's going on in their world at the time. A loving owner respects its a need for space, and that respect, over time, enhances the relationship and makes it deeper.

Cats seem to experience the world in a vastly different way than we do. While vision is our most important sense, it's much less important to cats. In addition, they have a radically different view of the world. Take a moment and get down on the ground, at cat level, and look around. The world is a vastly different place, and what lies beyond the hedgerow could be a driveway, a waterfall, or a chasm leading to a place far, far away. Imagine not knowing what lies around the next corner? Not knowing if what was there yesterday will be there today. Imagine if the world worked outside your control, how many walks would you have to take down that path before accepting the relative permanence and safety of the world beyond the big door.

Did you smell that? No? Your cat did. But maybe smell isn't the right way to describe what your cat experiences when he opens his mouth slightly and uses his tongue to guide additional odors, or components of those odors, to an olfactory organ in the roof of his mouth. Does a cat know how to get back home based on turning right at the yellow house, then left at the big stone with the cave-like cut out, or does he follow a scent trail of paint and lilacs and spore? What happens after a rain when the scent trail is washed away? When you walk in on your cat, dozing in the easy chair, and his ears twitch but his eyes remain sleep-closed, does he recognize the whisper of your slippers on Pergo or does the sound trigger his sense of smell? And what does that sense of smell mean? Does an impression form in your cat's head, a visual representation, a sensory one, or a full-on VR 3-D representation of you, the room, and the world beyond the big door?

I think of this, the way the cat's senses put him outside our understanding, as the cat world. We interact with our companions in the space where their world overlaps with ours. A temporal as well as physical coming together that resonates with us on an emotional level. And while we enjoy the time, at a subconscious level, we know that at any moment our cat might step back over the line into the cat world, closing us out until the next time our worlds overlap.

When you take your cat outside and he seems to have forgotten you exist, he ignores its favorite treat, the fishing toy dangled before it, and the scratch to the side of his head, don't take it personally. Your cat is fully in the cat world now, and all you can really do is wait for his return.

What is it about cats and their people? What is the source of the strange allure? Is it their dependent independence? Is it the magical purr? Is it the way they amuse us with their antics and play? Is it the silent meow? Or is it something more, something deeper, something more spiritual than physical? For me, it seems like a bit of all those things. But there's something else, something that I've felt time and time again; an affinity for the way they relax.

It may sound a bit strange, but think about the subtle joy and the loving jealousy you feel watching your cat relax. That languid stretch punctuated with a jaw-popping yawn. The methodical grooming of feline fur in a pool of sunlight on a chilly day. The unselfconscious curl into a relaxed ball. These activities give us pleasure, and maybe something deeper, a sense that this level of relaxation, this single-minded goal of comfort, is something we all aspire to.

This book is as much based on what my cats have taught me as what I've taught them. When you think about it, every cat knows how to walk and will do so, happily, without the burdensome harness and leash. The leash, to a cat, seems to denote the cessation of his being, a termination of the final escape route, a closing off of his ability to live in the moment. Getting your cat to accept, and then forget, the leash, is the goal. And though it could take weeks, or years, the walk is the practice.

Forget what you "know" about the cat and pick up on the truth through your day-to-day interactions. Your cat will tell you, loud and clear, who he is. You just have to listen.

Cat Walker: Bill Vander Zanden

Mr. Fix—it, Amateur Scientist, Outdoor Enthusiast, and Cat Walker

Bill Vander Zanden and his rescue cat, Kow, live near Chicago and enjoy regular walks in the neighborhood and shared time in the backyard. On YouTube, Zanden shares videos on everything from installing TV antennae to demoing how to use a power shovel.

At the time of the interview, Zanden had been taking Kow out for regular walks for about six years. "We'll often be out for 30-45 minutes most days, but sometimes we're out for six hours if I'm messing around in the yard. We often go out more than once a day. He rarely wants to come in."

Kow, a black-and-white domestic shorthair, was ten years old at the time of the interview.

Early Days

Kow came to live with Zanden when Kow was about four years old.

"I got him from my sister who worked with a rescue group. Cats come and go at her place; she fosters cats. Kow doesn't get along well with other cats, but he likes people and he sticks to me like glue." There's a fondness and respect that tinges Zanden's voice when he talks about Kow, revealing the depth of their bond.

"As long as you're not in a hurry, it's all good."
— *Bill Vander Zanden*

Training Days

Zanden began training Kow soon after he got him; Kow was four years old. Zanden initially bought Kow a harness, but Kow rolled around and managed to get out. "It didn't work for him, so I tried a dog collar that was more secure. Because cat collars have quick-release mechanisms, I felt safer with a dog collar."

Once he got a collar Kow couldn't wiggle out of, training him was simple. "He was pretty much trained from day one. I didn't have any trouble getting him to walk on a leash. He never really fought the leash, but he's perfectly happy to sit in the same spot for 20 minutes."

Following the Leader

When asked about the nature of their walks, Zanden explained that Kow likes to wander about on his leash. There's a park across the street from their home and they'll often end up there. "He moseys around slowly, sniffing at every little bump on the ground."

When asked who leads who, Zanden says he picks the direction but Kow sets the pace. "Kow will keep pace with me and then, suddenly, he'll stop and root around a bit. If we're going to the park, we kind of zigzag there."

In addition to the park, Zanden and Kow walk through the neighborhood and spend time in the backyard. "We both need to get out and enjoy the fresh air. We do that a lot. I'll secure his 40-foot retractable leash over a post in the garden so he can hang out in the yard with me."

Kow wants to go out for his walks, rain, snow, or shine. "No matter what the weather, Kow wants to be outside. If it's raining, he doesn't care, he'll stand in the rain. We'll walk even when the snow is 5–6 inches deep, but we'll stay on the sidewalk or walk in the street. We don't do that a lot because they salt the streets here, but he has no problem with the cold."

Tools of the Trade

Zanden uses a dog collar because Kow quickly figured out how to get out of a cat harness. He also uses a retractable leash on walks, which allows him to give Kow more range when something interesting crops up. He plans to reevaluate using a cat harness for safety reasons.

Cat-Walking Tip

Zanden says that if you're about to embark on leash training your cat, just go out and do it. "You don't know what your cat will do until you try."

WHY WALK YOUR CAT?

Before we delve into the question of why, we need to define what cat walking is. Cat walking, as opposed to dog walking, is not about taking your cat out to do his business, though some cats will. It's also not about getting your daily exercise, though it may augment it. Cat walking is not just something that crazy cat people aspire to.

Cat walking is about experiencing the natural world around you with one of its denizens at your side. It's about stopping and smelling and being in the moment. It's about exercising your cat's curiosity and his intellect. It's about your cat feeling the wind and the sun caress his body. And most importantly, it's about your cat learning to trust you as if you were his mother.

Your cat wants to go outside. He sits in the window, hungering for the hunt. He needs to taste the grasses and rub against flowers. He longs to feel the earth beneath its feet. He wants to feel the walls of his world push out, expand, and grow.

Cat walking isn't measured in kilometers or minutes. While you will enjoy it, much of that joy will be vicarious as your cat begins to trust the world and enjoy the walk for what it is, minute by minute, experience by experience.

Every cat is different, so while some cats will be sated by a walk around the block, others may be more comfortable with shorter, more controlled excursions. You've probably heard that walking a cat is not like walking a dog; the cat dictates the direction. That's only partially true. You can lead your cat, but there are places and situations that may provide too much stimulation for your cat, so you'll need to be cognizant of this. Sometimes just picking your cat up and carrying him past the object of its distress is enough, other times it might make more sense to alter your path. Either way, if you follow the directions outlined here, you'll be more in control of the direction, and in part, the pace.

Cat Walking Aids in Bonding

This is an interesting one, one that completely caught me off guard, but not for the reasons you might think. When I initially embarked on the task I had visions of my cat enjoying the weather, jumping at butterflies, and exploring the neighborhood. All of that happened, but took some time. First I had to acknowledge and help my cat get over some innate fears and complexities. One thing I had to understand was that my cat, being a small nocturnal predator, was also prey for larger animals. The fact that none of those animals were on my street made no difference; how was my cat to know? Putting a harness and a leash on him was akin to strapping a soldier into a straitjacket before asking them to walk through enemy territory. Every instinct was screaming "this is a bad thing."

It's positively terrifying.

But you have an ace in the hole. Beneath the terror is a place of curiosity and desire. Your cat needs to be out there. And while it will take time, if you're consistent in your practice, your cat will begin to feel more confident, and little by little, he will become less fearful. The cautious attitude may never go away completely, but the sounds, the smells, and the sights will become less ominous as your cat's practice progresses.

Somehow, I had to make my cat see that I was there to protect him, that I wouldn't let anything bad happen, and that even though his natural instincts were ringing off the hook, he was safe.

Without getting into the nature-versus-nurture debate, I'm here to tell you, it can happen. Cats want to be outside. They want to be a part of the natural environment. They want the stimulation. That's what makes it worthwhile. That's what makes it work in the end. All you need is time, patience, and lots of understanding, and your cat will lose much of his fear and put more trust in you.

Fear is part of what a cat is. It's a survival mechanism and, experienced in small doses, it's harmless and potentially beneficial. In the early days of cat walking (an indefinite term if ever there was one), your cat may experience an inordinate amount of fear. Even if nothing untoward and startling occurs, the sights, the sounds, and the smells are likely to be overwhelming. Your cat's senses will be on overdrive, and a short trip outdoors will likely leave him wiped out, wanting nothing more than to cuddle with you afterward.

That cuddle time is important. Your cat is seeking you out for affirmation, for love, and for understanding, so don't end your walk and dash. If you don't have time to be with your cat during the cool-down period after the walk, hold off until you do have time. If your cat hides from you after the walk, or runs as you approach, you may have overstimulated him. Give him a day or two to recover, and then try again, but rein in your enthusiasm. Make the next visit shorter and reduce the stimulation. Cats feel most comfortable in confined spaces. Boxed in. A fenced backyard is ideal. Being boxed in allows them to have a better feel for the space and gives them a sense of security that if danger does appear, they'll see it and have time to respond. Remember, with cat walking, slow and steady trumps speed every time, and soon, rather than running from you, your cat may decide to cuddle, thanking you for the terrifyingly wonderful trip beyond the big door.

Does that mean your cat is ready to take on the outdoors again? Yes and no. Your cat may cower from the thought of it, but a part of your cat really wants this, really needs it. Though, there's still that confinement of the harness and the leash to deal with—a condition that elevates but doesn't really trump the joy of the adventure. So even if you don't see it at first, it's there. I'm going to state this often in this book: walking a cat on leash is a practice, and even if your cat is having a bad day and refuses to budge from the crook of your arm, with each experience your cat is learning and growing. And even though your cat is happy, ecstatic even, to get back home, at his core, your cat enjoyed the experience. Its trust in you has grown. You have become an even more important part of his world. And just when you think you've gone too far, exposed your cat to too much too soon, he hops onto the windowsill to look out beyond the big door, processing, cataloguing, and comparing his experiences to what he sees from the safety of his window seat.

CAT WALKING PROVIDES MENTAL STIMULATION

Cats need more mental stimulation than can be provided for inside. I know some of you will disagree with this assessment, but while a fur mouse or a fishing toy can bring out the hunter in your cat, a bee, a butterfly, or grasshopper takes that hunting instinct and multiplies it by 100. Your walks, if you plan them right, can provide more stimulation than a box full of cat toys ever could. And while you'll need to rotate your cat toys to keep things from getting stale, you won't have the same problem with the sights and sounds beyond the big door.

The first time you observe your cat spot an insect, crouch down, and wiggle his butt in anticipation—an activity you've no doubt seen numerous times in your living room—you'll immediately understand the difference. The cautious demeanor it was experiencing just moments before will melt away, replaced with a steely resolve as your cat becomes one with the natural world. This is the real deal.

Don't get me wrong, the toys have their place. You should play with your cat daily, especially on days when you can't take him outside. But they are no more a replacement for the natural world than a travelogue is a replacement for travel. They both have their place, but beyond the superficial, they are worlds apart.

Even unwanted stimuli, such as cars, lawnmowers, dogs, and other people, will, over time, diminish in their impact. They will become part of the environment, something your cat may not like, but something he will begin to take for granted if you make sure that none of those stimuli result in negative outcomes.

And while it may be desirable to walk your cat on the sidewalk through the neighborhood, make time to do a little off-roading; take your cat into wooded areas where he can walk up and over and under and into places that demand exploration.

And remember, there's no scratching post as sublime as a tree.

Cat Walking Provides Exercise

This is probably obvious, but getting your cat out and walking is a great way to exercise your cat. Some cats even run a bit when they get comfortable walking on a leash. All you have to do is acknowledge their desire to pick up the pace and start to jog beside them. The first time you do it, your cat will likely freeze and look at you like you've lost your mind. While it's hard to know what a cat is thinking at any time, I'm pretty sure he thinks you're chasing it. Like he's prey. But then as your cat looks at you, he will realize he's safe, that it's just play, and within a few moments of the freeze, your cat will be jogging again. Some cats will enjoy having you at their side, keeping pace, while others will prefer you hang back a couple steps. But don't expect your cat to run until he drops. Cats are sprinters, not long-distance runners, so your cat will likely decide he has had enough long before you do. Respect that.

Carpet-and sisal-covered cat trees are helpful for sharpening and sloughing off nail casings; trees are better. A pot of cat grass may help your cat dislodge the occasional hairball or help his digestion, a yard full of grass gives him choice. A window seat may give your cat a window on the world; a walk through the neighborhood invites him into that world. It's the difference between looking at a photo of an apple pie and biting into a piping-hot slice.

This is the gift we all want to give to our cats. And we know, in our heart of hearts, that our cats want this too. Unless your cat received a lot of exposure to the world at a very early age, the window of discovery has shut.

It's time to open it.

Cat Walking Provides Safe Access to the Outdoors

Free-roaming cats face a lot of dangers and on average, live much shorter lives than cats who live their lives indoors. A well-fed and cared-for indoor-outdoor cat seems to have the best of both worlds at his disposal, and I understand the desire to provide that kind of life for your cat, because, in the end, I've no doubt the cat finds it ideal.

Unfortunately, it's not. There are just too many dangers out there: lawn chemicals, dogs, wild animals, and traffic to name a few.

Many cat owners, myself included, are a bit conflicted over the fact that cats kill birds and other native species. We applaud cats for keeping the rodent population in control and proudly brag about an especially good ratter, but when it comes to songbirds, not so much. To a cat, a bird is a rat is a mole; it's prey, and they indiscriminately take them to task. And since there's no way to say, "hunt this, not that," without your cat looking at you strangely, many of us overlook the occasional songbird carcass on the front porch. The fact that often, after killing the bird, the cat brings it to his owner as a gift also makes it hard to totally condemn the act.

But it is a problem, isn't it? Not for the walker or the housebound cat, but for the free-roamer.

Types of Walking Cats

Based on my experience and verified by the interviews I've conducted with others, there are three main categories that cats fall into when it comes to walking. While these groupings are distinct, they are really a continuum, so your cat may fall somewhere between groups. If your cat seems skittish one day for no apparent reason, remember that just because you can't identify the catalyst doesn't mean it doesn't exist. Our cats move in and out of our world, experiencing and processing their surroundings from a different vantage and perspective than our own. We are not cats and they are not us, despite our affinity.

Watching a cat pivot suddenly and sniff at a bush leaves me wondering if we really can grasp what's going on in their minds when they're taking in odor. On the surface, they're taking note of the passing of another animal, but the intensity and determination makes me wonder if more isn't going on here. It seems as if all of their senses have come into play. The cat seems mesmerized, unaware of his physical surroundings for a couple seconds as he decodes the message left there. How much information does scent carry? How does the Jacobson's organ come into play? Cats tend to use the Jacobson's organ even in instances when the smell is so strong that even us humans pick it up. If the organ was used just to amplify the scent, it wouldn't be necessary in many of the cases where it's used. Is taste involved? Do traces of images flutter through their brains, showing them who passed by this way? Or is it even more tangible than that, the equivalent of a head butt or an embrace?

A cat's sense of smell is better than our own by a factor of fourteen. When you think about it, that's so extreme that maybe it transcends what we think of as smell. Try to imagine what it would be like to have a sense of smell fourteen times more keen than the one you currently have. It would definitely be your superpower. Keep this in mind when you're out on a walk and your cat, for no apparent reason, stops and refuses to continue on.

We know that cats have an additional organ, the vomeronasal organ or Jacobson's organ, in the roof of the mouth. Cats, and other animals who have the Jacobson's organ, open their mouths when they're taking in a scent and seem to breathe in the odor. The action looks odd; as if the cat is in a trance as it stands immobile, its mouth open. This openmouthed pose is called the Flehman Response, and it's believed that it aids in identifying pheromones and the readiness of females to mate. Sounds logical, but invites the question, what else is going on here? How does this manifest in the cat's brain? Does it create images? Do they taste what they smell? Does it trigger an emotional response? What's happening when they use this additional scent organ?

We don't know, but we do know that it far surpasses what we take for scent. Cats do respond differently on different days. As illustration, the first cat I ever leash trained, Cougar, was a brave cat. He loved his walks so much that when he missed them he would pace around the apartment. The world beyond the big door was awaiting him.

On one walk I took him out and he immediately began pulling me down a row of cars. It was our usual direction, so I totally acquiesced. As we passed car after car, he continued on, until suddenly, he took a sharp right between two cars. When we got to the back of the cars, there was a dead rat on the ground. He'd smelled it from the moment we left the apartment and pulled me directly to it. It was amazing and opened my eyes to a whole new world I wasn't a part of. But that's not where it ended; on windy days he was, if not downright skittish, hyperalert. He seemed to be responding as if signals were coming to him from all directions at once, and he couldn't get a handle on what was going on. It was so pronounced that even though he wanted to go out, I usually avoided our walks on windy days. While windy days were verboten, after a rain, he was generally a little subdued. It was as if the rain had washed away many of the ghosts of the past and cleared the environment of many of the signposts and byways of this other cat world.

So back to categories of cats. The three types I alluded to earlier are:

- Grazers
- Observers
- Trotters

While their names reveal a lot, let's dig into each and what it means to you.

GRAZERS

While most cats like to eat grass, Grazers spend more time moving from blade to blade than most. The world is one big salad and they want to make sure they get their share. A sunny patch of grass on a mild day is often enough to keep grazers entertained. In fact, for some of them, this is the walk.

Grazers often prefer to hang out in a thicket of grass rather than explore the neighborhood. These cats will often, after eating their fill, decide to sit down in the grass and relax, enjoying the sun, the sounds, and the smells. The walker spends much of the time standing or sitting beside the cat holding on to the leash in case the cat is startled or another animal enters their space. As a walker, this is the perfect time to read, knit, write, or drink a nice cup of tea or coffee. This is a time for both of you to enjoy sharing space and time with each other. Rather than seeing the fact that your cat isn't much of a "walker," enjoy the wonderful opportunity to just be with your cat. And while grazers don't get a lot of exercise, they get the necessary mental stimulation and pleasure from being outside in nature. Can you turn your grazer into more of a trotter? It's possible and a worthy goal, as long as you can show your cat that getting a little exercise is fun, too. But don't expect your cat to give up grazing completely. You may be able to reduce its need to graze, not replace it. The first step in redirecting your grazer from its single-minded determination is to purchase a pot of wheat grass from the grocery store or pick up a pot of cat grass from the pet store. Your cat will appreciate it, and if it always has fresh grass available to it, it might not spend so much of its time grazing on your trips outdoors.

Caution: All Lawns Are Not Created Equal

To keep your cat safe, make sure your cat doesn't eat grass that's been treated with harmful fertilizers, pesticides, or herbicides. When out walking your cat, look for the tell-tale signs of a recent lawn treatment: visible chemicals on the lawn or surrounding sidewalk, a wet lawn that may have just been treated, or lawns so green and weed-free that they look artificial. In addition to ingesting chemical-laden grass, your cat could get poisoned from licking the chemicals off its fur and paws. If you suspect your cat walked across a treated lawn or through a tainted area, immediately clean its paws and coat with a damp cloth upon returning home.

OBSERVERS

Observers like to investigate every crack and crevice in their environment. Some will want to cave; they'll want to get out of sight and observe their world from a protected space. Of the three types, this may be the most fearful and the most difficult to acclimate. Observers often love window seats in the home, where they can safely observe the goings on of their world without interaction. These cats generally benefit from longer real-world acclimation periods. Your challenge will be to encourage your observer to become a more active participant. Start small, meaning short five- to ten-minute walks where you don't let the cat cave, but encourage movement and exploration. Success with observers often results in cats that are less fearful around company and more likely to join in on the fun.

TROTTERS

Cats are not dogs. I can't stress this enough, but trotters, as their name implies, trot. These cats seem to have someplace to go and getting there is half the fun. They tend to be more social cats, cats who don't mind meeting strangers or being petted by people they don't know. This is the smallest group, but the most visible, as owners of trotters are more likely to continue the training process and their walks. Trotters generally take to walking on a leash much quicker than cats in the other two groups. But like all cats, even trotters will have days when they don't feel nearly as social or brave. The world around them dictates their mood more than dogs and you should remember that even trotters like to stop and smell the roses from time to time.

If you've already begun training your cat, you've probably already decided which type of cat you have. But here's the thing, just like people, cats can and do change over time. As you read through this guide, I'll provide you with tips that will help you mold your grazer into something more akin to a trotter. But while your cat is capable of changing groups, it generally takes a lot of time and patience before this will happen.

CAT WALKER: CAROLYN OSIER

CAT BREEDER FOR 45 YEARS AS WIL-O-GLEN CATTERY, PUBLISHED CAT WRITER, CFA ALLBREED CAT JUDGE, RETIRED SPANISH TEACHER AND TRANSLATOR, AND CAT WALKER

Carolyn Osier breeds CFA award-winning Abyssinian cats and has trained more than one of her cats to walk at her side. Twenty years ago, she decided to train a very gregarious Abyssinian named Barnum. His people-loving personality made training him to walk on a leash a foregone conclusion.

At the time of the interview, Barnum is no longer with us, but his spirit lives on.

TRAINING DAY

Osier decided it was time to leash train Barnum when he was six months old. "He was a natural meeter and greeter," Osier explains, "and he wasn't afraid of dogs."

Osier is one of the lucky ones; Barnum seemed born to walk on a leash. "It only took a couple of days to train him. As soon as he realized that he could go out, investigate, and meet dogs and people, he took to it right away."

FOLLOWING THE LEADER

Osier and Barnum would take a walk out to the mailbox, take a tour of the pool area, and explore the neighborhood. A couple of their more unusual trips included a cat show at the mall and to a dinner held by a rescue group.

In all cases, Barnum led, yet Osier made suggestions. "You can't force a cat to go where you want it to. You follow where it wants to go. I kept pace with him. When I'd suggest a new direction, a conversation ensued. He would sometimes decide, okay, that direction looks interesting. Other times, not."

Tools of the Trade

Osier used a cat harness with Barnum. "I prefer the ones with Velcro closures, though I've used harnesses with clips. It's easier to adjust the Velcro harnesses. I had a Velcro harness that was hand sewn by a seller on the Internet. As long as you can secure it around the neck and chest, it should work. Once, in an emergency, I used a ferret harness."

Osier stresses the importance of getting a good cat harness before embarking on the training. "Figure 8 and dog harnesses aren't safe for cats."

As for leashes, Osier uses standard fabric and leather leashes. She goes for the shorter, 5-foot leashes.

"When you purchase a pedigreed cat, you have some idea of what kind of a personality you're going to get. Abbys are cats that are out and about and enjoy exploring. More inquisitive cats are better at the leash walking experience."

—*Carolyn Osier*

Cat-Walking Tips

Osier says the tricky part is getting your cat used to the harness. She suggests you put the harness on and leave the cat alone. Initially, it will be paralyzed. After a while, it will decide it can walk with this thing on and eventually become comfortable with it. Once that happens, you want to put them in a situation in which they have things they like to see. Let them explore, and they will.

"Don't train," Osier explains. "Give them the opportunity to watch what's going on. With all of the Abyssinians I've ever worked with, three minutes into the procedure and the cat is ready to walk."

Osier believes that pedigree can separate the walkers from the window seat inhabitants. "When you purchase a pedigreed cat, you have some idea of what kind of personality you're going to get. Abbys are cats that are out and about and enjoy exploring. More inquisitive cats are better at the leash walking experience."

When asked if there was anything else she'd like to share about her walking adventures, Osier gave this piece of sage advice: Never let them take your credit card.

Zazen: The Meditative Cat

"If we had the consciousness of a cat or a dog, we would have it in us to become perfect Zen masters. We could gnaw on a bone, take a nap, play with a spider until we killed it, get our litter just right, and be innocently and serenely present. Meaning would mean nothing to us, nor would we need it to mean anything. We would be free, and we would be spared. But, we are human beings, and we possess that odd duck—human consciousness."

—*Eric R. Maisel, PhD*

Do cats meditate?

It sounds like a foolish question on the surface, one intended for books with less serious aspirations. The questions is not intended to raise eyebrows, but consciousness.

It raised mine.

It began with my consideration of the cat's purr, that magical rumble that seems to come from within, that doesn't appear to require a breath, and seems to be the physical manifestation of pleasure.

Science has dissected the mechanics of the purr in an attempt to figure out how our cats make the sound. Oddly, the jury is still out. The most popular theory, described in Wikipedia as speculative, goes something like this: Cats use the vocal folds or the muscles of the larynx to rapidly dilate and constrict the glottis. This causes vibrations when the cat inhales and exhales. Combined with the steady breathing of the cat, purr happens.

Some of the literature describes this theory as fact, but it is neither the only theory nor the first. In the end, we're just not sure.

If the literature is to be believed, we have a better handle on why cats purr. Our understanding, based primarily on observation, is hampered by the fact that we are not cats and can only hypothesize on what's actually going on in the cat's mind. Still, there's no denying the purr of a happy cat. His joy and calm are palpable and undeniable and his nonstop rumble makes people happy. There's no doubt in most custodians' minds that with their purr their cats are professing their love.

Maybe it is. Maybe not. It turns out that cats also purr when they're dying or incredibly ill or anxious. These conditions, love and death, are pretty far apart. Could something more complex be going on here? Are there other situations where cats purr that aren't as apparent?

There's also a more cynical theory that the cat's purr is a form of manipulation; they realize its impact on us so they use it to keep us providing food, comfort, and shelter. I'm not particularly fond of this hypothesis, partially because I'm a cat fan, but more importantly, I don't know how anyone could test this. Unlike love, which is impossible to define but easy to feel, this one doesn't pass the sniff test.

Some people believe that a distressed cat will purr to calm itself, not unlike a meditator chanting a mantra or listening to his breathing to refocus attention away from discursive thoughts. Why would we be the only animals to benefit from meditation? Make no mistake, much cat behavior is enigmatic. Every cat I've ever owned was an individual and exhibited at least one behavior that was outside the species norm. Researchers do their best to prove their hypotheses, but in the end, cats hold their most important secrets close.

One of these secrets is its purr.

As I began to seriously consider the connection between mantras and cat purrs, I thought about my own meditation and the fact that my cats are attracted to me when I meditate. That led to more corollary observations, which in the end, led me to believe that cats are the ultimate meditators.

Keep in mind that we know very little about our cats and the world they inhabit. They seem to have one foot in our world and three feet in another; a world of sight and sound and smell that we're not privy to. And more and more I realize that the things we know about cats, the things we take for granted, are not necessarily the full story.

As a writer and someone who used to live alone, I probably have more quiet time than the average person. And over the years, every cat I've ever owned seemed to respond to that quiet. For instance, the first cat I owned after moving out on my own was a gray cat named Grey Gray. Grey Gray was a big love bucket, but he was not a lap cat. Except, of course, when he was. He would only sit in my lap when I was at my desk, engrossed in a creative project on my computer. At those times I was mentally gone, buried beneath the weight of my creations. I wouldn't see him, but I'd feel him as he climbed into my lap. He would join me in that space outside of place and time and he would rest his head on the back of my left hand and partially close his eyes as I worked. It made typing difficult, but he was so relaxed and happy that there was no way I'd move him. It was shared time, and despite making it hard to type, it was wonderful. One thing you'll hear from cat owners, over and over again, is that they get "stuck" in one uncomfortable position or another solely to accommodate a cat that has joined them in their repose. Their cat will climb on them and become so relaxed that their owner will become transfixed and literally unable to disturb their cat without feeling a strong sense of guilt. Even the most people-centric cats need their time and space away, and will ignore your cries for them to join you in your world. When they come to us, step out of their world and into ours, it's always a special time and many of us alter our plans to accommodate them.

Zip forward about a couple decades to one of my current cats, Elinor. Elinor is a small Bengal, no more than seven pounds, and she has a gentle but skittish demeanor. She loves me, but I'm way too tall and ungainly for her, so when I go to pet her she runs. Often, though, she'll climb her five-foot cat tree, closer now to my height, and solicit petting from there.

I began working from home and allowing Elinor her space. I installed climbing shelves for her (which she adores) and limited my petting to the bare minimum, stopping well before she got overstimulated. To say that these concessions worked is an understatement. But back to the reason for this diversion; when I'm engrossed in work on the computer, Elinor climbs up on the coffee table behind me and taps me on the back so I'll turn and give her attention.

I think that focus, the all-in nature of writing or studying or creating is as close to meditation as most of us get. When I'm totally engrossed in a project, I go into a state similar to the calm of meditation, and my cats want to be a part of that. It's kind of like a melding, like we're sharing a stream of calm.

So okay, they like calm. But that's not meditation, right?

Right. I'm getting to that. You see, just like our cats, we're attracted to their calm, too. Watching a cat languorously stretch out a paw, yawn, and go back into that calm place makes us feel good. We often envy the completeness of their calm, their ability to let go of the day's accumulation and just be. Something we find so hard to do, except when we're engrossed in an activity like creating, studying, or reading.

The purr as mantra.

Think about it.

Then think about sleep. Cats sleep up to 16 hours a day, but much of that sleep is light. In an article on cats and sleep in the March 2015 issue of Tufts University's *Catnip* newsletter, Dr. Beaver, former president of the American Veterinarian Medical Association, said: "Early on, they [cats] had to hunt for food to stay alive, and that desire for food can require a lot of energy. So sleeping helped cats conserve their energy. Even though the common house cat does not have to hunt for its next meal, a cat is still conditioned for sleep. House cats sleep a lot more than feral cats do because they don't have to spend a lot of time searching for food." However, a portion of this sleeping time—perhaps as much as 40 percent—is spent resting and not in deep sleep, according to Dr. Beaver.

Forty percent. Resting. That's an awful lot of their sleep time where they're not really sleeping. Is that period more akin to a meditative state? Could it be that cats slip in and out of a kind of meditative state that we can only dream of? A prolonged, restful state where the world goes by, observed, but not joined, while they fully relax?

It seems likely. Remember, much of the research on cats is inconclusive. We can only dip so deep into the cat world before we realize we're in over our heads. So often studies are littered with words like "might," "may," and "can," qualifiers that illustrate our inability to know for certain what our observations mean. The best material on cat behavior comes from those writers and researchers whose research subjects are their own cats. Cats only share glimpses into their world with the people they love and trust. A love and trust that takes months, or years, to earn.

So, when I say I think our cats may be the ultimate meditators, it's based on the truths my cats have shared with me and the uncanny sense of well-being and calm I get from watching a cat "sleep."

Cats Shouldn't Be Walked

You'll hear this from time to time from well-meaning cat owners. This usually happens during the early stages of your practice when your cat's fear has gotten the better of it and it's attempting to hide, refusing to budge, or trying to get out of its harness. I have come to believe that most of these people, at one time or another, failed miserably at cat walking.

Don't fret; though the comments are often dismissive and rude, they are well-intended. They think they're looking out for your cat. They think they know your cat better than you do.

But they're wrong.

Walking on a leash is about as abnormal as living in a house or apartment, and cats are pretty good at that. But not at first. Bring a new kitten into your home and it's likely to spend much of its first few days hiding.

But most, unless they're feral or have been mistreated, get over it in a few days. Because they're malleable, time and hunger help them through the process. Unfortunately, unless you're planning a camping trip under the stars, your cat is unlikely to get more than an hour of outdoor time per day, unlike its trial by fire in the house. Also, the house is a controlled environment. There aren't as many scary sounds, animals, cars, or machines to deal with. In the house, your cat can run back to its safe place if frightened. When on leash it's imperative that you become your cat's safe place. You can't do that if you're dealing with your own stuff, if you don't know how to slow down, quiet down, and just let things be. If you respond to your cat's fear with anger or disappointment you'll impede its progress, and in most cases, fail.

Make no mistake, the failure will be all *yours*.

Yes, they're independent, but not nearly as independent as their ancestors. They depend on us for food, a warm and safe place to sleep, and companionship that crosses species lines.

When a well-meaning person tells you that walking your cat on a leash is somehow unnatural, tell them that taking your cat safely outside, in your control, is about giving your cat access to the natural world and meeting some of its needs denied it by its housebound existence.

Fear

Your cat's level of fear is an important consideration and should be taken into account as you work through the process. Let's get one thing straight—all cats can be taught to walk on a leash, but the type of walker they become is based on life experiences, genetic factors, and the type of cat walker you are.

My cat Puma was diagnosed as being extremely shy. The first couple of days with Puma were rough; he cried pretty much non-stop and refused to eat, drink, or play. On the third day, I took him to my vet for his initial checkup and after a couple minutes of observation she told me that in her twenty years of practice she had never seen a more frightened kitten. She even went so far as to put it into his medical records. I went home with something to calm him down as it was important that the little guy begin to eat and drink. It didn't seem to be working, but at about three a.m. the next morning, as he began his hourly crying jag, I pulled out a feather toy and tried to get his attention, something I'd done dozens of times with no success. This time was different; he suddenly stopped crying and playfully batted at the feather.

When I began walking him, I realized I had to do this slowly and methodically. I lived across the street from Golden Gate Park, so I alternated walking him in the neighborhood and the park. He was about six months old, so his kitten curiosity and fear were battling it out. The fear always won, but something strange happened. When we would go inside, he'd seek me out to cuddle. Every time. I initially thought that it was because he was still scared and needed me to feel safe again. I believed this for quite some time, but one day while walking a trail in the park, he went into what I call bliss mode. He stopped in his tracks, looked up at me adoringly, and then began twining around my legs and kneading the soft earth of the trail. It was so extreme, almost like a catnip high.

I realized that despite his fear, he loved it outside. In a sense, how could he not? Much of the fear a cat feels is more a claustrophobic reaction to being on the leash. With a leash on, he can't exercise his innate need to flee in the face of danger. All you have to do (but don't) is unleash a scared cat and watch its confidence level rise. He may still seek out a protective bush or a spot under a car as a safe lookout, but once he realizes the coast is clear he will begin to explore.

So how do we get past this innate need to flee?

1. Never punish your cat. You should represent safety and love, not fear. When your cat misbehaves, the solution is often to find an alternative that your cat prefers. A cat that likes to scratch needs multiple acceptable scratching materials. Never use a water bottle or a loud sound to "train" your cat to leave the furniture alone. I'm no saint, I realize this can be hard, but punishment doesn't work and can negatively change the dynamics of the relationship.
2. Engage in lots of hand-holding. When your cat is afraid, pick him up and carry him in the direction you were going when the fear occurred. Or sit down on the ground so you're at your cat's level and encourage him to sit in your lap until whatever it is he fears is no longer a threat.
3. Reward your cat for bravely moving forward and making progress. Use an audible "good kitty!" a calming pet on the head, and a treat. Initially, your cat won't respond to these

rewards as his senses will be overwhelmed by the scents, sounds, and sights that surround him. But the accolades are getting through; your cat just doesn't have the bandwidth to respond to them. One day, when you least expect it, your cat will take the offered treat or arch up into your palm as you brush your hand across his back. Then you'll know that he's starting to habituate on some of the sights and sounds of the neighborhood and feels more confident.

After six months of practice, my clinically shy cat has made an enormous amount of progress. He still doesn't want to walk through the neighborhood, so I pick him up and carry him about half a mile from home. He trembles from fear, but when I set him down he begins the walk home. He goes quickly for the first couple of minutes—he'd run if I let him—but I remain calm and walk at a regular pace. Then, a few minutes into the walk, he slows down and his tail comes up confidently. He stops, looks up at me, and purrs. I reach down, and he raises his head so that I can pet him as he kneads the ground. It's a rather stunning turnaround as he goes from fear to complete bliss mode in a matter of minutes. He then enjoys his walk home, frequently stopping to get petted while circling my legs and kneading the ground. He is still a fearful cat. But walking and facing his fear has resulted in a braver, more confident cat whom I'd categorize as a trotter. Even his fear of people, which used to make him flatten himself on the ground in abject terror, is no longer a foregone conclusion. In fact, he even used to do this when we approached a house with people in the yard or garage. Now, most of the time, he'll pick up the pace a bit and bravely pass by. He still doesn't like it when people approach, so I simply pick him up and walk on. When I first started doing this, he used to hide his face in the crook of my arm, but he hasn't done that for quite some time.

He is learning, bit by bit, that most of the stuff that he finds scary really isn't. I sense that he's already learned that lesson, but hasn't gotten over the knee-jerk reaction. I have a feeling, by the time this book reaches you, he will have changed again and the sight of people approaching will no longer cause him undue stress.

Research on cat bravery implies a strong genetic component in how brave a kitten is that can't be easily breached by early socialization. While it's virtually impossible to separate nature from nurture, if nurture were the gating factor, we could raise all kittens to be brave little soldiers. The truth is, these experiments have resulted in kittens that fall at various points along the continuum. Keeping this in mind, some kittens may require a quieter, less public walk. You must allow them more time to acclimate to an area, and potentially keep to a single location for all of his walks. Given enough time, you may be able to expand a fearful cat's domain, but it must be on the cat's terms. What does that mean? Go slow. Pick your cat up whenever he crouches or tries to hide. Carry your cat until he feels confident enough to want down again, which, after a while will be surprisingly quick.

My cat Puma was a fearful cat and he's now a trotter. That's an extreme change for a cat who came into the world as a clinically frightened kitten. I've watched his confidence grow, both inside and outside the house, in lockstep with our practice. I don't have enough data points to come out and declare that cat walking is a cure for a frightened cat, but in Puma's case, it was. He's still not a demonstrative cat; he doesn't greet company, but no longer hides from them. He might even take a treat from an outstretched hand. And his walks, while they still start out fearful, end with him experiencing full-on bliss. Pretty heady stuff if you ask me, and much worthier of research than a lot of the studies being done today. Puma is not done learning. The practice continues, and I know, with each walk, his fears decrease a tiny bit more.

Understanding cat fear can be helpful in dealing with it. Remember, our companions are pretty low in the food chain, so they must be cautious to survive. When your cat chooses to hug a hedgerow or climb in or under things, keep this in mind. Coax, don't demand. Pick up, don't pull. Keep moving forward when your cat experiences unnatural fears. If your cat decides to cover his head in the crook of your arm, let him. In time, he will raise its head. Curiosity will prevail. Don't expect it to happen overnight. Just like meditation, it takes some rewiring. Your cat has to feel safe with you. You must become his rock. He must believe that your presence changes everything.

Just as changing your focus and quieting your mind takes a lot of practice, so does getting over fear. Don't think of the process as a staircase with equidistant steps because it's not. There are many staircases to navigate—some going up, some going down—until you reach the garden path and the way levels out.

PART I
BALANCE

In this part, the groundwork for the training is laid. Harnesses, leashes, and other tools of the trade are discussed.

Harnesses, Leashes, Collars, and Pet Chips

Harnesses

Most people suggest you use a harness when walking a cat. Cats can often back out of a collar unless it's uncomfortably tight. In addition, cat collars are designed to break away when your cat gets caught on something. Ever see a cat get the handle of a paper bag caught around its neck? The cat will totally flip out and run through the house at breakneck pace, bumping into people, furniture, and walls. No matter how you try to calm him, he usually won't stop until the bag is dislodged, he reaches a dead end, or he becomes winded.

It's an extreme claustrophobic response, one that you should keep in mind the first time you put a harness on your cat. Most cats won't feel as trapped as they do with a bag around their neck, but they will react nonetheless. The most common response is immobility. Your cat may stand motionless or even fall over on his side as if suddenly stricken. Other cats will flip around, jumping in the air as they try to free themselves from the harness.

Harnesses come in a couple styles. The more traditional style, the nylon figure-H harness, uses adjustable webbed bands that you clip around the cat's torso. While figure-H harnesses are often easier to find and cheaper, they do require a bit more fiddling to get the fit right.

The other style, the walking jacket, looks more like a piece of clothing. It's a fabric harness that secures with industrial-strength Velcro or plastic clips and comes in a number of materials, colors, patterns, and styles. While neither is foolproof, they are much more secure than a collar and when properly fitted the failure rate is acceptably low. Once your cat gets used to wearing a harness, escape will be less of a concern. When choosing a harness, look for one that comes in multiple sizes. Some harnesses are "one size fits most," which tend to fit best on average-sized cats and may not work with small or large cats.

While I prefer walking jackets, if you are training a small kitten you may have a difficult time finding a walking jacket that is small enough. H-style harnesses are more adjustable, just make sure you find one made for kittens. While dog harnesses can often be used, there are now a wide assortment of harnesses made with cats in mind. My advice would be to stick with a cat harness.

When fitting a harness, make sure it's snug. You should be able to slide one to two fingers between your cat and his harness. Too loose and your cat will be able to back out of it while on your walk.

Harnesses designed for dogs can work, but it makes more sense to get one expressly made for cats. There are a number of online vendors that sell cat harnesses if you can't find a suitable one in your local pet store.

Finally, once you've completed your walk, take the harness off. Harnesses don't break away like cat collars, so don't leave a harnessed cat unattended.

Leashes
Selecting a leash is dependent on your cat and what type of walker he turns out to be.

Ribbon
Traditional ribbon leashes are available in an enormous variety of colors, weights, and materials. When selecting a ribbon leash, find a light one made from a cotton or nylon material. These are among the cheapest options and are best suited for grazers, cats who are more interested in grazing than exploring. Your cat is more likely to get tangled up in this type of leash.

BUNGEE

Bungee leashes are a cross between ribbon and retractable leashes; these cloth leashes have in inner elastic core that scrunches up the leash and expands as the cat moves away from you. This provides a similar "get out of the way" benefit as a retractable leash, but doesn't provide the control as to when or how far the leash extends. Bungee leashes are best suited for cooperative, secure cats who don't spook easily. Bungees can be used effectively with trotters and secure observers.

RETRACTABLE

Retractable leashes are typically longer than bungee and traditional cat leashes. These leashes often expand to 6, 10, or 16 feet when fully extended. In most cases, you won't need one that's longer than 10 feet.

These leashes extend on an as-needed basis, allowing you to give your cat more leeway to explore or rein him in to gain greater control. Most retractable leashes have a lock button so that you can lock the leash at a comfortable length.

Aside from being able to control how far your cat can stray at any given time, retractable leashes are slack-free so your cat is less likely to get tangled. This is especially helpful if your cat likes to start and stop a lot, as do observers.

But there is a major consideration when using a retractable leash. You must be careful never to drop it! If you do, the handle will fly toward your cat and cause him to run from it, mindlessly, terrified, as though his life were in danger. A cat in this state will run right into traffic without looking. If you're lucky, the handle will get caught on something and stop his progress. This is so serious that I almost suggested against using this type of leash, but with care and caution, you can make it work.

That said, you can avoid this problem by creating a wrist strap. If the handle is dropped, it will still be connected to you. To do this, I created a chain of elastic hair ties and looped one end around the handle and the other around my wrist. This works wonderfully. If the leash slips from your grasp, it hangs about six inches from your hand. Not only does this avert disaster, but it also frees both your hands when you need to pick up your cat because unleashed dogs (or poorly controlled children) enter the vicinity. Because hair ties have a definite lifespan, I make two chains. That way, when one of the ties breaks, there's a backup so that it doesn't go careening after my cat and scaring it out of its wits.

Because of their slack-free nature and greater control, retractable leashes are an appropriate choice for all three cat types. I use a retractable leash with all of my cats. Please exercise extreme caution if you decide to use a retractable leash.

COLLARS AND PET CHIPS

Your cat should always wear a collar with an ID tag. In addition to the ID tag, you should get your cat chipped by your veterinarian. While the ID tag will be your first line of defense, a cat collar is designed to break away. If your cat gets caught on something or manages to get its collar off, chipping your cat provides an important fail-safe. A chipped cat that ends up at the vet or a rescue center can be reunited with its family.

Cat walking marginally increases the possibility your cat will need to be rescued. Despite our best efforts, many cats are good at working their way out of harnesses and collars. Your cat may become perfectly content wearing his harness, and it may even provide an extra sense of security when outside. And then one day your cat sees something he wants or is startled and he pulls on the leash, backs up, and wiggles free. In a matter of seconds, you go from a pleasant walk to a heart-pounding chase through the neighborhood! To avoid this, always make sure the harness is properly fitted and in good repair. If it's not, your cat will notice, and under the right circumstances, he will take advantage of the situation.

That being said, one of the benefits of walking your cat is that the cat now has a strong sense of home and is able to home in on it with near preternatural ease.

Remember, collars should never be used to walk a cat; their use is as a carrier for an ID tag.

Cat Walkers: Dale Robertson and Paul Rigo

Dale Robertson: Senior HR Systems Analyst and Project Lead, Flea Market Investigator, and Cat Walker

Paul Rigo: Corporate Manager – Oncology Services, Collector of Art Nouveau Antiques, and Cat Walker

Dale Robertson and his partner, Paul Rigo, have been walking their cat Sophia since she was a kitten. Sophia, a doted-upon silver ticked American shorthair, was 2.5 years old at the time of the interview. They made it clear that although she doesn't walk like a dog and doesn't seem to get the distinction between the sidewalk and the street, she's a pretty good walker.

Early Days

Sophia didn't require a lot of training. For her, learning to walk on a leash was pretty natural.

"We started with the harness. After getting her used to wearing it she became interested in going outside," Robertson said.

As a precaution, they had her chipped before taking her outside. The first trip outside, they held her, letting her get a taste of the outdoors without pushing her too quickly. Next, they introduced her to the front porch, and then stepped down on to the sidewalk.

"She didn't really wander, but she was very interested in her surroundings," Robertson said. They realized at that point that they needed to buy a leash.

While she doesn't walk like a dog, Dale and Paul have seen improvements over time.

"She enjoys her walks, but she does get distracted by things like blowing leaves. We can usually get her back on track," Robertson says.

"People love it when they see her out on a leash."

—*Dale Robertson*

Following the Leader

Leading a cat may be the Holy Grail of cat walking. It's something many walkers aspire to, but few accomplish. "I can lead her a little bit. She knows what it means when I tell her to 'come.' I coax her and talk to her and she'll let me lead for a bit."

In addition to their neighborhood, Dale and Paul walk Sophia in an RV park association that leads to the lake where Dale and Paul can sit with a good book and a good cat tethered at their sides. "Sophia is right at home and doesn't fear the people and dogs that saunter by," Rigo says.

On some days, they tether her out in the backyard so that she can enjoy the weather and wander about her yard. And finally, down the street is a cat café that serves snacks and places cats that need a forever home.

TOOLS OF THE TRADE

Sophia wiggled out of the first harness they purchased for her, so they bought one with secure clips that's worked much better. "If she sees a bird or a squirrel, she may try to bolt, so we needed a secure harness."

In addition, they use a retractable leash for greater control.

CAT–WALKING TIPS

Robertson: Let the cat set the pace. Dog walking is for exercise and using the bathroom, but with a cat, it's more about letting them explore.

Rigo: Let them get used to the harness first, and then clip it to something in the yard so they can explore their own yard before you venture out.

Aerial Dog Runs and Mobile Tie-Outs

An aerial dog run is a cable strung about eight feet above the ground, between trees or buildings. A tie-out cable is attached to the aerial cable with a swivel clip and the other end is attached to your cat's harness. It provides your cat with a range of motion while at the same time teaching your cat that there's a limit to its wanderings.

Getting your cat used to an aerial dog run is a great way to begin his outdoor adventure. A cat on an aerial dog run gets to go out and be with the family and enjoy more freedom.

As part of your leash-training plan, you should incorporate the use of an aerial dog run and/or a mobile tie-out. By using these tools, your cat will learn that when he gets the end of his leash he can go no farther and must alter his direction. Unlike a walker, the tie-out never bends, so there's no negotiating and inconsistent messaging. The more you use these tools, the more cooperative your cat will be when out on a walk. In the beginning, you'll need to let your cat lead, but as soon as your cat gets comfortable enough to start tugging on the leash to go in a different direction, it's time for you to become the lead! Hold your place when your cat comes to the end of the leash. Your cat will not pull as much and in most cases, will alter direction, allowing you to lead your cat. Be consistent and don't give in. As soon as you do, your cat will realize that persistence works and you'll find it difficult to redirect your cat. Of course, there will be times when you can't resist, your cat is reaching for something it wants to explore, something it was meant to do. In those cases, don't give slack; instead take a step in the direction the cat is headed so that he can reach his goal without tugging on the leash.

When purchasing an aerial dog run, select one designed for small dogs. Aerial dog runs made for larger dogs have tie-out cables that are larger and use heavy clips that will be uncomfortable and difficult for your cat.

When using an aerial dog run there are a few things to keep in mind:

- Never leave your cat unattended while on the tie-out
- Make sure your cat has access to water and shade. If not, limit the time and avoid hot days
- Locate your run so that there are no obstacles that your cat can wrap himself around; that way, you won't need to constantly untangle your cat

Because the use of an aerial dog run requires a yard with enough space to install an aerial cable, it's an optional part of the process, but one that may have far-reaching impact on the walker and his cat. If you live in an apartment or a community that doesn't allow you to make modifications such as this, you can still train your cat using a mobile tie-out.

CONVERSION TIP

Alter the length of the tie-out cable so that there is very little slack. This will reduce your cat's lateral range, but it will also keep the cable from tangling on items in the yard and around your cat's legs. An even better solution is to replace the tie-out cable with a retractable leash. Simply use a plastic tie to attach the retractable leash to a swivel clip. So now, instead of using a tie-out cable, I pull out the retractable leash and attach it to my cat's harness. Because it's taut, my cats rarely get tangled around stuff or their legs tangled in the cord.

MASTER TIP

My dog run was fine, but the clasps on the tie-out were a bit bulky, more appropriate for a medium-sized dog than a cat, so I purchased a 10-foot cat tie-out cable to replace it. This was shorter than the included tie-out, but turned out to be the perfect length. The tie-out barely touches the ground and allows about two feet of lateral movement.

Make Your Own Mobile Tie-Out

A mobile tie-out is a great solution for those who can't install an aerial dog run. The problem with most tie-out options is that they require you to put a stake in the ground or tether the tie-out to a stationary object like a tree. That doesn't allow much flexibility and cats get bored quite easily if you don't allow them to move from one spot to another.

A mobile tie-out provides flexibility and offers the following benefits:

- Provides a simple way to tie your cat out in the yard
- Your cat learns that when he comes to the end of the leash that's as far as it can go in that direction, this aids in teaching your cat to follow your lead in cat walking
- Move from place to place easily and quickly
- Share time with your cat while working outside
- Perfect for vacations, camping, or other outdoor events
- No stake to set
- Can be used indoors or outdoors
- Take it with you wherever you go

Here's how you can make a simple mobile tie-out. You will need:

- A full or empty paint can. You can buy empty paint cans at your local hardware store or paint store.
- Stones, dirt, or play sand.

- A 10-foot tie-out cable. Find a tie-out cable that's made for cats or small dogs so the swivel clips and cable are not unwieldy for your cat.

To Build a Mobile Tie-Out

1. If you're repurposing a full can of paint, skip to step 4.
2. Fill the can with ballast; play sand, river stones, or dirt.
3. Put the lid on and tap it down with a rubber mallet so that it doesn't come off.
4. Clip one end of the tie-out to the handle and the other end to your cat's harness.

Now that you've created a mobile tie-out, you can use it to keep your cat near when you are working in the yard or just providing your cat with basking and exploring time. If you don't have your own yard, you can take it to a park, a clearing, or even on a camping trip and keep your cat safe and in your control while he enjoys the outdoors with the family.

Unless you've got a large yard, keep the cable short so that you're not constantly untangling your cat. The problem with traditional tie-outs is that once you've either staked them into the ground or tethered them to a stationary object, moving the tie-out to another place is something of a chore and there are areas where it won't be easy to anchor it. The mobile tie-out provides limitless opportunities for your cat to explore.

Important: Never leave your cat unsupervised while tethered to a mobile tie-out. Your cat could get tangled and hurt, or another animal could enter the yard and attack your companion.

ZAZEN: PRACTICING PATIENCE

"Zen is not effort. Effort is tension, effort is work, effort is to achieve something. Zen is not something to achieve. You are already that. Just relax, relax so deeply that you become a revelation to yourself."

—*Osho, mystic, guru, and spiritual teacher*

Understanding that your cat is as much a prey animal as it is a predator is the first step in creating an empathetic bond with your cat. This bond is somewhat elastic, and if you're dependable, it will continue to grow throughout your cat's life. That being said, bad behavior can be detrimental to the bond, so much so that you should not try to train your cat if you are impatient, under a considerable amount of unaddressed stress, easy to anger, or prone to losing your empathy when things aren't going your way. If this is you, you may want to focus on establishing a regular meditation practice before focusing on teaching your cat to walk on a leash. Give yourself a few months of working through some of your own frustrations before taking on the challenging task of cat training.

Throughout this book, we focus on Zen, or more explicitly, zazen, which means "seated meditation." Zazen is just one path you could choose. There are numerous types of meditation, and any meditation technique you choose will help you find your place of calm. While meditation is not required in order to train your cat to walk on a leash, patience is. Without it, you're not likely to succeed.

I do not practice Zen Buddhism, but I've explored it along with various other flavors of meditation. I have adopted a practice that is neither one nor the other, an amalgam of things that have worked for me. If you're new to meditation, you'll find that most forms are similar and do not conflict with or require adherence to religious doctrine. In a sense, all meditation has a similar purpose; to quiet the mind and help you achieve a level of inner peace.

If you become a meditator you may find that not only has it helped you in cat training, but it will have the corollary effect of deepening the connection between you and your cat, you and your family, you and your friends, you and your job, and you and yourself.

CAT WALKER: ERIN O'NEILL

MYSQL DATABASE GEEK, PHOTOGRAPHER, DRAG QUEEN, AND CAT WALKER

Erin's cat Jaxon Binx, an Oriental Shorthair kitten, is the first cat she's successfully trained to walk on a leash. He's also the first Oriental Shorthair she's ever owned. She got Jaxon when he was six weeks old and she immediately began acclimating him to the leash. She attributes part of the reason for her success to the  fact that she started very early, but she also feels that there are some cat breeds that are more likely to learn to walk on a leash.

Erin and Jaxon Binx have a very special connection, one that sometimes falls outside the norm. O'Neill, who is on the Asperger's spectrum, believes that may have something to do with the uncanny communication she shares with her cat. They sometimes communicate without words or meows. A kind of knowing. "Once, an image of water filled my head. I noticed Jaxon Binx staring at me and then his empty water dish."

Their deep communication provides a level of empathy and compassion that, no doubt, aids in Jaxon's training.

EARLY DAYS

O'Neill wanted to take advantage of the brief window when kittens are known to be most adaptable. She began leash training Jaxon Binx the week he arrived. "On the first day, he seemed very cold, so I made a little covering for him from the sleeve of a child's sweater. I cut off a length of the sleeve and then cut little holes in it for his legs. He got used to it pretty quickly. So when I put the harness on he was already used to wearing the sweater so he readily accepted it. He wore it for hours because I forgot to take it off."

On day two, O'Neill put the harness back on and attached a leash. Jaxon Binx began walking around the apartment, on leash, on the second day of training.

"I think some pedigree breeds make better walkers than others."

—*Erin O'Neill*

Following the Leader

Jaxon Binx took to the harness and leash in no time, but he's still getting his sea legs when it comes to walking outside. At the time of the interview, most of their walks were in the backyard, but she had plans to take him over to the neighboring High School and Dolores Park, a heavily used park in San Francisco's Mission District, where on any given day you're likely to run into a variety of San Franciscans, dogs, exotic birds, iguanas, and a smattering of tourists.

While the neighborhood park is a goal, O'Neill knows she has to work up to it. Fortunately, the breed is known for loving their people, and Jaxon Binx is no exception.

"Right now, I let Jaxon Binx lead, except when it comes to steps," O'Neill says. She explains that even though she lets him lead, if he heads in a direction that's dangerous she'll give him a little pull to stop him and use a wand toy to encourage him to change directions.

Tools of the Trade

O'Neill uses a puppy harness and a retractable leash with Jaxon Binx.

Cat–Walking Tips

O'Neill offers up a simple tip for people who want to follow in their footsteps: "Start early. The earlier you begin, the easier it will be for your cat."

TREATS, TOYS, AND BEHAVIORS THAT MAKE YOUR CAT HAPPY

What toys make your cat crazy happy? What treats can he never get enough of? Identify these, stock up, and save them for behavioral rewards.

For cats that are motivated by treats, they can be offered as encouragement when your cat decides he doesn't want to walk anymore or insists on going in a different direction. Pet your cat and then offer up a treat. Hold the treat in front of the cat so he has to step forward to reach it. Then move back, and offer another. Keep this up until your cat begins walking in the appropriate direction again. In the beginning, your cat will be preoccupied with all the sensory information he's receiving and ignore the treat. That doesn't mean you shouldn't try. After you return home and take off the harness, give your cat the treats he refused while out on the walk.

For cats that aren't food motivated, a favorite toy can be wiggled in front of them, encouraging them to move toward the toy. Call for your cat as you shake the toy. Just as with the use of treats, he probably won't be swayed in the early days of its practice.

If your cat won't come when called, turns down the treats, and ignores the toy, it's time to pick up your cat. Carry your cat a good six to ten feet and then put him back on the ground. That is often enough to get many cats moving again.

Age and Leash Training

To say that age is important is something of an understatement. The problem is, many people believe it's an indictment, damning adult cats as incapable of learning. Adult cats are much more difficult to train than kittens, make no mistake, but in most cases, it's not impossible. Time, patience, and love are amazing tools—keep your arsenal well stocked and even the most sedentary cat will reward you.

How old is your cat? Age, while not a qualifier, can be an asset. The earlier you expose your kitten to the outside world, the easier it will be for your kitten to adapt.

Kittens should be introduced to the outdoors as soon as your vet gives you the okay to do so. You can't start early enough. Young kittens are still learning the rules of the world. Novel experiences are imperative during the formative weeks if you want to help your cat adapt to new and different experiences as it ages.

Even before you get the okay to take your kitten out into the big world, invite as many people as possible over to meet your kitten, positively interact with it, and provide rewards such as treats. Try to incorporate men and women, men with and without beards, kids and adults, people of varying races, and those who love as well as those who don't like cats. This will go a long way in socializing your kitten to different types of people.

Also, take your kitten on short trips in the car. To the drive-through, the park, to friend's homes, etc. Always pack his favorite treats and toys and lavish him with treat-filled activity. Don't be alarmed if your kitten ignores the food and/or toys at first, just keep at it. When he starts to play or eat the treats, you know you're making progress.

For older cats you'll also want to expose them to as many novel situations as possible. If your adult cat wasn't well-socialized as a kitten, these excursions and visits might be overwhelming at first. For instance, if your cat doesn't want to interact with your friends, take his favorite snack or toy and save it exclusively for interactions with friends and family. Let them offer up the treat, rather than you. If he won't take it from them, ask them to call the cat's name and wait until they have his attention, and then place the treat on the floor and walk away. If he doesn't take the treat while they're in the house, pick up the treat and put it away for next time. Once your cat realizes the treat leaves with the guest, your cat may come up with the courage to take the treat the next time a guest visit. If you do this enough, your cat will begin to look forward to company because only good stuff happens when company arrives. This could take a long time, especially if you have company infrequently, but it's definitely worth the effort.

Cat Walker: Harriet Crosby

Writer, Wannabe Decorator, and Cat Walker

Harriet and her cat Killian, a beautiful flame point rescue, live in a gated community backed by a golf course. The golf course attracts a lot of wildlife, including deer and a myriad of bird species that Killian enjoys stalking from the safety of his leash.

Killian was five years old when the interview was conducted.

Early Days

Killian was about a year and a half when Crosby decided it was time to train him to walk on a leash. Crosby began by acclimating Killian to the harness. After Killian got used to wearing it, she began taking him out on her deck. "At first we'd stay out for five minutes or so, then ten minutes, and then, when Killian became comfortable on the deck, I began taking him downstairs. I took him out in the dawn or predawn because there were fewer cars and people about."

For several days Crosby let Killian explore the area surrounding her unit. After about a month, they worked their way around to the golf course behind her building.

She began going out later and later, gradually acclimating Killian to people and cars. Today Killian doesn't even get upset when they encounter a dog. "He still gets a little nervous at loud cars, but he's pretty good any time of day now." With the golf course behind their home, Killian gets a lot of stimulation and enjoyment from stalking the wildlife and exploring the open space. "He loves the sand traps. He digs into them up to his shoulders and then goes somewhere else to do his business."

When asked if Killian is still improving as a walker, Crosby said: "No, I don't see continued improvement or any backtracking. Once you've conquered the fear of people and cars you're at the apex of cat walking. That's it."

Following the Leader

"You hold on to the leash and let the cat lead. When it's time for personal grooming, he stops and does it. When it's time to lie down, he lies down. He loves to sniff the undercarriage of cars. That said, sometimes I do a little bit of leading; a bit of pull-pull on the leash to get him going in a different direction. When it's time to go home, I pick him up and take him in."

Tools of the Trade

"I used a 22-foot retractable leash so that Killian can climb trees on the golf course, which is something he really enjoys. He feels like he's BMOC when he does that."

Crosby uses a harness with clips, but isn't really a fan. "I don't like the clips as the harness shifts about a bit. Killian is a big cat, so when he gets frightened or feels he has to get away fast, he does a Houdini and gets out of the harness."

Cat-Walking Tips

Crosby says that cat walking truly is a Zen experience. "There is no purpose and no expectations about how long you'll be out or what you'll do. You do it so the cat can go outside safely and won't be able to harm songbirds. The only reason to do this is to let them go outside safely and to protect the environment from them. That's the only reason to train your cat to walk on a leash. I have no notions that we'll be walking downtown Walnut Creek. If he wanted to or had more fortitude, fine. The cat is built to do certain things, so give that up. Cats are not dogs, cats are cats."

ON MEDITATION

Crosby has been meditating for five years now. She doesn't believe in setting expectations. "I don't think it does anything; it's just what you do. When I start putting expectations on my meditations it becomes a disappointment. All I do is show up."

How Manageable Is Your Cat?

How easy is your cat to handle? When your cat is frightened, does he cave into you or does he totally freak out and try to get away? Does nestling your cat in your arms calm him down?

If you have a young kitten, make it your task to pick him up and touch his feet and his belly multiple times a day. Give him a treat after you play with him so that your kitten builds a positive association with being handled.

If your cat feels safe in your arms, this will aid in your cat-walking practice. If your cat hates being held, you will need to work to get him over this. Believe it or not, it's possible, but, as with all things related to cats, it takes time.

I had a cat who hated sitting in my lap, but loved me to run my nails down his spine. So every time I picked him up and put him in my lap, as he moved to jump down I immediately began scratching his back. An important thing to note is that I didn't try to stop him, I just scratched his back. The first couple times he paused, and then jumped down. Each time I did it, he stayed a little longer. Once I got him to stay for a bit, I extended the time by offering a treat when he tired of the back scratching, and kept him in my lap a little longer. Over time, I could pick him up and pamper him a bit. It didn't turn him into a lap cat, but he stopped fighting me over it. On our walks, if I need to carry him, he may do a little complaining and a little struggling, but then he calms down and accepts it. As with all training, it's better to withhold treats between training sessions. This doesn't have to mean he gets fewer treats, just that they're saved for rewarded behavior. Teach your cat to sit, and every time you want to give it a treat (for being cute or sweet), tell it to sit, and then give it a treat when it follows through.

THE OUTDOOR CAT

If your cat is currently an outdoor cat that you're trying to convert to an indoor cat, you have your work cut out for you. You're asking an animal that has had a taste of complete freedom to accept the limited range of the leash.

If possible, convert the cat to an indoor-only animal first. Once it's settled into its new indoor existence, it's time to begin leash training. I'd highly suggest the use of an aerial dog run or a mobile tie-out to help with the transition. Once your cat realizes that in order to go outside it must be wearing a harness, it may accept the harness and leash readily. Despite the fact that your cat is used to the outdoors, it will still need to get over the fear of being on a leash. Past experiences will likely have been riddled with incidents where it cautiously avoided potentially dangerous situations, ran from other animals, and was startled by sights and sounds.

Based on your cat's past experiences and personality, the amount of time it will take to train your former outdoor cat may be nearly as long as training an indoor cat experiencing the outdoors for the first time.

Step 1: Acclimating Your Cat to the Sounds of the Neighborhood

As part of the process, your cat will need to get used to the sights, sounds, and smells of the neighborhood. Sounds, especially loud, harsh, city sounds can be difficult for your pet to get used to.

Create a Neighborhood Soundscape

Take a walk through your neighborhood and record the sounds. You will be amazed at how a relatively quiet neighborhood can harbor so many sounds that your cat is likely to fear. On a typical day in my neighborhood, my cat is exposed to the sound of traffic, sirens, sweeping, lawn mowers, human chatter, hedge trimmers, garage doors opening and closing, dogs barking, etc. Most of these sounds will be new to your cat. A half an hour should be sufficient, but feel free to record as much as you'd like. Keep in mind that the more variety you capture, the more effective it will be. Try collecting sound at different times of the day and on weekends and weekdays to collect the widest variety of sounds.

After creating your soundscape, play it in the background when you're playing with your cat or feeding it. This will quickly become routine, and your cat will come running when he hears the sounds, eager for his play session or his meal. I suggest playing it at least once daily, more if possible. You want your cat to be familiar with the sounds of the neighborhood when you finally do venture out.

While acclimating your cat to the sounds in advance will help, it won't completely mitigate his fear the first time your cat encounters the source of the sounds. For instance, if you take your cat for a walk and he's already used to the sound of a garage door opening, it will still likely freak your cat out the first time it sees one open. Trust me, if your cat wasn't already acclimated to the sound, your cat's response would be even worse. When you return inside, turn on your recording with the garage door sound and either feed your cat or bring out his favorite toy. Do this every day and the next time your cat encounters a garage door, it will be a little less frightening.

Note: The author has created a number of SoundWalks that will save you the trouble of creating your own. For information, see http://www.cliffordbrooks.com/soundwalks/

Step 2: Harnessing Up

Once you've decided on a harness, it's time to get your cat used to it. Cats don't take easily to anything confining. While YouTube will have you believe that cats will wear virtually anything, it just isn't so. In fact, you may be surprised at how extreme your cat's response is.

Many people suggest you get your cat used to the harness over several days. On day one, they want you to merely drape the harness on your cat, letting him get used to it just lying on his body for a few minutes. They suggest you do this over several days before actually putting it on him and attaching the Velcro or snaps. There's nothing wrong with this procedure, but it may be a little unnecessary. Rather than go through this, I suggest you show it to your cat, let him sniff it, and drop it on the floor and leave it there for a while. A day should be more than enough time for the cat to accept it as just another part of its environment, but in most cases, you can get away with a few minutes. Your cat, in smelling it, has pretty much decided it's benign.

Now it's time to put it on your cat. Hold it up to your cat and then adjust it. The first time your cat wears it, it doesn't have to be securely fitted, you just want to make sure it's tight enough to keep it from falling off. The first time you put it on, I'd suggest doing so either when the cat is in a playful or a sleepy mood. If your cat is the kind of cat who is hypersensitive to change, choose the sleepy, meditative time. If your cat is still a kitten or a playful adult, pick playtime. In either case, talk softly to your cat as you put the harness on. Don't give in if your cat fights it, just put it on. Your cat's initial response might be to jump around a bit, bite the harness, or become immobile. Keep talking softly to your cat and as soon as it calms down, offer it a treat. After the treat, it's playtime. Kittens and cats with a high prey drive will likely forget all about the harness within minutes. Some cats may take longer, but keep at it, and your cat will come around. Play with your cat until he begins to tire, give him another treat, and then let him continue to wear the harness for another hour or two.

More on Treats

Whether you're teaching your cat to respond to his name, teaching him to use the toilet, or teaching him to walk on a leash, treats are your strongest tool. Once you know what your cat's favorites are, it's time to redefine your relationship with treats. It may be hard at first, but to be effective, you'll need to limit your cat's favorite treat to effectively reward him for a desired behavior and create a positive association. That doesn't mean he'll get less; in fact, during the training process he's likely to get significantly more.

While some cats respond favorably to "Good boys!" and "Atta girls!," not all do, or, maybe they do, but unlike humans they don't see it as a motivating factor. The way to many a cat's heart is through his stomach. A hungry cat will be more motivated, so when possible, schedule your training before mealtime. If you free feed, consider changing to a scheduled mealtime so your companion isn't always full. I'm not advocating withholding food or starving your cat, I'm merely suggesting you use the time before a meal to your advantage.

There are some people who associate treats with junk food and don't like to give many to their companions. It's true, treats are not meal replacements, but as long as you don't give them handfuls at a time, you should be fine. Also, there are a number of healthy treats on the market. They may be a bit more expensive, but should address the health concerns. That said, just like human treats, the less healthy alternatives may be the ones your cat loves. You may need to experiment with several treats until you can find one you both can live with.

A side benefit to identifying and judiciously providing treats is that when it's time to pill a cat, often, you can hide the medicine in with its treats.

Step 3: Leashing Up

Once you've acclimated your cat to the harness, getting him used to a leash is straightforward. Like the harness, the first thing you should do is place the leash on the floor beside your cat. Your cat will examine it, smell it, and in short time, decide it's benign and go about his business.

Get your cat's attention again and then pick up the leash and manipulate it in your hands. If it's a retractable leash, you will want to pull it out and let it retract (slowly, not by itself) a few times, so your cat can hear the sound. Then, before your cat loses interest, place the leash on the floor beside your cat again. Your cat will likely do a little more investigating, just to make sure his initial assessment was correct. Now it's time to clip the leash to your cat's harness.

After clipping it on, give your cat a treat. The leash will confuse your cat, so you'll need to go slowly. If you're using a retractable lead, be careful it doesn't slip from your grasp at any time. A clattering retractable lead is scary.

Now, pick up the leash and follow your cat around as he walks around the house. If you've taught your cat to sit, tell him to sit. Reward your cat for sitting and let him get up and walk around some more. Every minute or two, tell him to sit, and reward him again. After your cat has done this several times, stand your ground and let your cat walk to the end of his leash. When he gets there, say "sit," and give him another treat. If he doesn't sit, and pulls, no worry, this is a good time to find out if the harness is secure as he will be likely to try to wiggle out. If he seems to be succeeding, adjust his harness and begin again.

Once you're sure the harness is fitted properly and you've given your cat enough time to begin ignoring the harness, you're ready for your first trip outdoors.

PART II
PRACTICE

Your cat will face both his fears and his desires head-on as he ventures beyond the big door. At the same time, if you're up for a similar challenge, you'll begin a regular meditation practice, taking what you've learned so far and facing your own fears and desires.

Step 4: The First Trip Outside

Okay, the big day has arrived. You've been playing your soundscape tape during your play sessions, you've gotten your cat over the tyranny of the harness, and you've walked your cat through the house on leash.

Take a deep breath. No, not a meditative one, but a literal one. This is the day all your dedication has led to. It's time to venture beyond the big door.

Begin by harnessing your cat. Take a moment to ensure the fit is right; snug, but not tight. There should be enough room to slide a finger or two between harness and cat, but not so much that your cat will be able to escape.

Now attach the leash. Offer up a "good kitty," and give him a preparatory treat to prime the kitty pump. Next, walk toward the door, backward, coercing your cat with another treat to follow you while keeping the leash slack. When you and your cat near the door, pick up your cat and cradle him in your arms as you open the door. Be prepared to reposition your cat if he gets frightened and tries to claw his way back inside. If you think this may be your cat, you may want to wear a jacket, just in case. Don't worry, if it's a warm day you can probably take the jacket off once you've crossed the threshold.

As you step outside, your cat will immediately be bombarded with a sensory dump. Sun and fresh air. Sounds swirl about you. Trees wave, leaves skitter, and a whirlwind of odors fill your cat's consciousness, only a small subset of which you will be aware of.

Take another virtual breath—deep and fulfilling—and set your cat on the ground. Choose a grassy area, preferably near some plants, that's surrounded by a fence or shrubbery. Sit down on the ground beside your cat. If your cat climbs in your lap and hides, that is a good thing as it means your cat sees you as a source of protection. If your cat begins to explore or sample the grass, that's also a good thing. In the end, one is not better than the other, it just is. It's a reflection of where your cat is at that very moment.

If your cat decides he wants to explore, get up and follow him.

If your cat is scared, keep the first outing to no more than 10 minutes. If your cat is exploring, grazing, or interested in what's going on around him, play it by ear. If something scares him, pick him up and see if you can calm him down. If you can, put him back on the ground and let him explore some more. If he's still scared or returns to you for security, it's time to go in.

If nothing seems to be bothering your cat, you should stay out as long as he is enjoying the outing. You probably are one of the lucky ones who has a cat that came into the world ready to explore. While this is a very small percentage of cats, they're out there. The rest of the training will be abbreviated for you, though the practice never ends. Whenever your cat feels ready to take the next step, let him.

If your cat tries to go somewhere unsafe, or you need to impede his progress, hold your ground. Do not pull your cat back to you, instead, hold your ground so your cat can't go any further. If your cat digs in or plants himself on the ground, it's time to pick him up and move him to a different location. If he returns to the same spot, pick him up again. Keep doing this until he decides that maybe he doesn't want to go there after all.

So what do you do if the unthinkable happens: a snarling dog rounds the corner, a car backfires, or a bicyclist catches your cat off guard? Your cat will likely freak out, jumping and pulling at his leash, flipping over and about, trying to get to safety wherever that may be.

Virtual breath time. Remain calm. This is where your cat shows you his contortionist skills, and if you're not careful, he will escape the harness. Move toward your cat as he will be trying to back out of the harness, and quickly bend down and scoop up your cat. Don't stress. Don't be afraid of your cat, but keep his flailing claws away from your face. Carry your cat away from the source of his fear and place him on the ground. He may cower or begin to pull again. If he does, sit on the ground, consoling, treating, and loving your cat. Do this before taking him back in. While you may be shaken up too, don't show it. The fear your cat felt is acceptable fear. He will get over it quicker than you will if you remain calm.

Welcome to the world of the small predator.

As your heartbeat returns to normal, keep in mind that your cat's response is due to the fact that he couldn't escape the situation. If he hadn't been on leash and had the freedom to flee, the histrionics would have been at a minimum and recovery would have been much quicker. When danger approaches, cats generally flee. Danger is normal, being tethered isn't.

But there you were to protect your cat. On a certain level, your cat understands that you won't let anything bad happen to him. That doesn't make the instinct to flee any easier to ignore; only time and experience will do that.

Now that that's out of the way, let's be honest. It's not likely anything untoward will happen on your first trip out, but it's wise to be prepared because eventually, something like this will happen. As a cat walker, you'll need to be vigilant so that you can head incidents like this one off at the pass.

When you bring your cat in, immediately take the harness off. You will no longer put it on during playtime. Your cat needs to understand that when you put the harness on, it means you will be taking him on an adventure.

ZAZEN: BREATHING

"When you breathe in, swallow the whole universe.

"When you breathe out, breathe out the whole universe.

"In and out.

"In and out.

"Eventually you forget about the division between breathing in and breathing out; even breathing is totally forgotten.

"You just sit with a sense of unity."

—*Maezumi Roshi, Zen Buddhist teacher*

Most forms of meditation require you to focus on your breath. Often the breaths are modulated and you are asked to breathe from the navel, inhale and exhale for a count of eight, or engage in other activities that require a learning curve and a lot of practice before you can reap the benefits. It can be difficult to create a rhythm that's not your own.

With zazen, you are instructed to breathe normally. There's no work involved. No straining to extend the breath. You just breathe as you normally do.

And count.

Not the length of your inhales and exhales, but rather the number of them. As you breathe, you count each breath, counting from one to ten and then start over again. There's nothing magical about the number ten; you're just training your mind to let go of discursive thought patterns and the emotional baggage that comes along with them.

Initially you count both inhalations and exhalations. While it sounds easy, in the beginning you're not likely to get very far before your mind throws up some noise that distracts you from the task. When it does, simply acknowledge the thought and let it go. Redirect your attention back to your breathing and start the count over again at one. Don't be dismayed if immediately after dismissing one thought another intrudes. Let that one go too, and start counting your breaths again. Don't think of the count as a goal, but like a metronome, helping you keep in sync with your breathing. In time, you will get better and better at it, but don't expect to reach ten very frequently at first.

What's hard for most people to accept is that even when the thoughts continuously intrude, they're making progress and benefiting from the practice. When you dismiss the thoughts, you are learning how to let go and to deenergize the thoughts that take up so much of your waking hours and lead to destructive levels of stress. Each time you let a discursive thought go, you've managed to neutralize the impact it has on you.

After you feel you've made some progress, only count the exhales. At first, it may feel like you've taken two steps back as it now takes twice as long to get to ten. But I found that doing this, taking this transitionary step, helped me focus more tightly on my breath and away from the count. The less you enlist the mind, the easier it is to keep it quiet.

Try not to think about the counting, just do it, and after a while the counting will fade into the background, indistinguishable from the breaths, and at that point, you can stop the counting altogether and just focus on the breaths. When thoughts intrude, acknowledge them, let them go, and return your focus to your breaths.

The goal is not to completely stop thoughts altogether; thoughts are the by-product of a healthy mind. The intent is to stop discursive thoughts from taking over; thoughts that have a storyline or a repetitive theme. Flashes of thoughts are okay, don't worry about them, just refocus on your breaths.

If you have trouble focusing on your breaths, count them again. What you are trying to do is stop the mind from racing and going to disturbing or anxious places, not stop thinking. Part of what Zen provides is a path to a life where anxious thoughts don't rule you. Even benign thoughts, when they capitalize on your consciousness, make it difficult for the important stuff to surface. So when the thoughts seem to have a hold on you, remember that each time you dismiss one you've moved a small step forward in your practice and in quieting your mind.

Return to the breaths.

While it may not seem like you're stilling the mind by counting the breaths, as you continue, you will experience times where the count fades and you are in the moment, experiencing it purely, without any thoughts. These moments will be fleeting at first, and some days they will seem impossible to attain, but don't despair. Like anything, the more you do it, the better you'll get at it. Don't beat yourself up if you have a good day followed by a few "bad" days. This too, is normal, and evidence that you're still growing and learning to manage your thoughts.

The noisy days will happen from time to time, well into your journey, but things are not the same as they were when you first started. You will have changed. Your mind will be more in your control and even though it may seem as if the thoughts are burying you alive, stop and ask yourself the following questions:

1. How long did it take for you to realize the thoughts had returned and you had lost track of your breaths?
2. How difficult was it to let go of the thoughts?
3. How did you feel? Was the emotional content of the thoughts less intense than before?

If you've been meditating for a while, the answers to those questions may help you see that even on your noisiest days, the impact of your practice has changed the way you respond to the noise, and that's a huge and important change. Something to celebrate.

As an aside, much of the benefit of meditation is realized over time. There will be subtle changes in your demeanor, how you deal with stressful encounters, and how quickly you recover. The things that bother you will soften and change, and others—family, friends, coworkers—may recognize the changes in you before you do.

But it takes time, and each of us is different. Give yourself the time you need, acknowledging that change will happen but it will be subtle at first and easily overlooked initially.

When in doubt, breathe.

STEP 5: THE SECOND TRIP OUTSIDE

The second trip should be much like the first one. After harnessing your cat up and checking the fit, take your cat to the same place you went to on your first trip outside, unless you had a bad experience there and are worried it will happen again. If it was a fluke, take your cat to the same location, as you'll need to detoxify it by replacing the bad memory with a better one. If there is a chance of a repeat, take your cat to a more secure location for its second outing.

The second trip may be rougher than the first. Even if nothing bad happened the first time out, there is so much new information to take in that your cat may be focusing on totally different stimuli. That said, follow the steps of his first trip out and set him down in the same spot. Remember, your cat's senses are much greater than yours, and there's no way you can take in the totality of your cat's experience. Everything is new. Everything is a potential danger. Everything is exciting. And your cat is unable to habituate on anything. It's overwhelming, but even if your cat doesn't appear to make any progress, or appears more fearful than the first day, your cat is collecting experiential information. Information, over time, that will allow it to separate the fearful from the routine.

You're on your way.

Cat Walker: Jesse Nyland

Human Rights Advocate, Poet, Animal Lover, Group Facilitator/Speaker for LGBTQ Community, Parent of One Human and Two Feline Children, and Cat Walker

Jesse Nyland and his 16-year-old Bengal, Xena, began their walking practice in earnest after Nyland decided to enlist the services of Xena as a therapy cat for an assisted-living facility. Xena, he explained, is a people person. The prospect of going to see her friends at the assisted-living facility was the catalyst for a major change in her walking practice; suddenly, she looked forward to her constitutionals more than ever and what had been an off-again/on-again walking adventure became a regular part of their lives.

While many cats shy away from strangers, Xena loves to meet people and enjoys it when they stop to admire her. And dogs? While not exactly a fan, they don't bother her as they pass on their walks. "She has a personality all her own," Nyland said lovingly.

EARLY DAYS

Nyland first began working with Xena when she was about one and a half. He began using a collar rather than a harness, which he deems a mistake. "She would stop and lay down when I tried to walk her, and she would try to back out of the collar."

Nyland says that switching to a harness made a huge difference for Xena. "Because it wasn't around her neck, like the collar had been, she was much more comfortable."

Their first walks took place in his apartment as he got her used to the reality of the leash and the harness. After he got her used to walking on a leash indoors, they braved the world beyond the big door.

"I let her lead first, but then I give her a gentle tug and redirect her. I take control of the remainder of the walk; she goes where I want to take her."

—*Jesse Nyland*

TRAINING DAYS

During her training, Nyland would seek out places that Xena would be interested in going. She was afraid of traffic so he steered clear of it. "Once we were out," Nyland said, "the distraction of the place was enough to make her forget all about the harness. Each time we went out, she became more comfortable with the harness."

Nyland feels the key to their success was that when he took her out, they did what she wanted to do. "She really has approval over the time we spend outdoors. She likes to see people, so I take her out where she will likely encounter people on our walks."

FOLLOWING THE LEADER

When they begin their walk, Nyland lets Xena lead. They live next to a park, so when he sets her down he lets her pick the initial direction, but he keeps her on the path. "The more I took her out, and the more often she got to go where she wanted, the more eager she became about her walks. I let her lead first, but then I give her a gentle tug and redirect her. I take control of the remainder of the walk; she goes where I want to take her."

That said, when they walk, Xena often tries to take over the lead. If she stops or tries to go in a different direction, Nyland will give a little tug and redirect her. She ignores rabbits and birds; when she's out in the park she doesn't get distracted. She's too busy making progress. If she gets tired, Nyland picks her up and carries her for a while.

TOOLS OF THE TRADE

Nyland's cat-walking equipment includes a padded harness with clips and a standard leash. He prefers a standard leash so that Xena's distance from him is always the same.

Cat-Walking Tips

When asked for tips on training your cat to walk on a leash, Nyland had a few:

- Make sure you have a comfortable harness for your cat. Nyland prefers padded harnesses and walking jackets to the plain straps.
- Figure out what your cat likes and take it to places it will enjoy.
- Stay away from things/places that scare your cat.

He also feels it helps to start when your cat is still a kitten. Growing up, he had a Siamese cat that loved going places in the car and riding in his bicycle basket. He loved spending time with his people.

Final Thoughts

Nyland told me that he felt that providing the extra stimulation of a walk is important in exercising your cat's intelligence and providing exercise. He feels that taking them out of their environment and exposing them to other things and places is important. He believes that you should provide your cat, both inside and outside the home, with things to jump on and a variety of things to stimulate them mentally and physically.

Before the interview ended, Nyland shared a painfully funny joke: "I named my cat Cigarette because every night I put her on a leash and take her out for a drag."

Ouch!

ZAZEN: SITTING

"You should sit in meditation for 20 minutes a day, unless you're too busy; then you should sit for an hour."

—*old Zen saying*

TIME OF DAY

You're probably familiar with the full lotus position. Most of you have probably attempted it at one time or another and either failed miserably, screamed in pain, or reveled at your flexibility as you easily (look, Ma, no hands!) slid into position. Fortunately, there are a number of acceptable positions that will allow everyone to find a position that's comfortable.

But why the positions anyway? What if you're not interested in the ritual aspect of zazen, or any type of meditation for that matter? Can you still practice zazen sans trappings? Good questions. First, the goal of the various positions is to adjust the body to clear the breathing path so that the breath comes effortlessly. There's also an emphasis on comfort, so the positions have been designed to remain comfortable for long periods of time. Even the full lotus, which for those of us without the flexibility seems harsh, was designed to be stable, balanced, and allow you to sit for long periods without discomfort. So while you don't necessarily have to select one of the positions outlined in this section, you should be able to find a comfortable one.

EQUIPMENT

Fortunately, you don't need to go out and purchase much to begin meditating, but you'll find that using a couple meditation pillows will aid in aligning your spine and increasing the amount of time you can sit comfortably.

A zabuton is a rectangular pillow designed to cushion the meditator's legs and knees while sitting. Think of it as your meditation mat.

To assist in maintaining a straight spine, many people use a zafu. A zafu is a round meditation pillow. The meditator sits on the edge of it, elevating the pelvis above the knees, which helps to align the spine and distribute the meditators weight. You can use a zafu with or without a zabuton, but they are often used in conjunction. Use of a zafu also helps in positioning the knees so they are touching the zabuton or the floor.

CLOTHING

Choose something loose fitting and comfortable. Often, people meditate in pajamas, sweat suits, and yoga wear.

THE POSITIONS

BURMESE POSITION

In this position, your legs are crossed and the feet lay flat, the upper surface of the foot is flat against the zabuton or floor. The knees should also contact the floor. If you're having trouble positioning your knees, a zafu may help. Sit on the first third of the cushion and adjust your weight until your knees are flat on the zabuton. At first, this may cause a bit of strain, but over time your muscles will relax and it will come much more easily.

HALF LOTUS POSITION

In this position, the legs are crossed and either the right foot or the left foot is on the opposite thigh. The foot should rest back near the crotch; the other foot should be laid flat against the zabuton. This position can cause an unbalanced feeling in some and you should switch which leg you place on the thigh from time to time.

FULL LOTUS POSITION

In this position, the legs are crossed and the feet are placed on the opposite upper thigh. This is the most stable position of all, as it assists in aligning the spine while creating a stable platform for meditating. While this may be the most stable position, it's no better than the other positions as for as the actual meditation goes. If you find this position uncomfortable or it requires your attention while meditating, use a different position.

SEIZA OR KNEELING POSITION

This position doesn't require a zafu. In this position, you sit back on your heels with your knees on the zabuton. If you don't want to place your weight on your heels, you can also purchase a seiza bench which will allow you to maintain the same position without having to sit on your heels.

SITTING IN A CHAIR

Finally, you can sit in a chair. The best chairs are straight-back so that your spine is kept straight. Your feet should be flat on the floor.

OTHER CONSIDERATIONS

MEDITATION MUDRA

The meditation mudra is a hand gesture used during meditation. When seated in any of the traditional meditation positions, your hands should form a mudra. The mudra used in Zen forms an oval. The right hand rests on top of the left with the fingers of the right hand cradled by the fingers of the left. The thumb tips come together and touch, forming an oval.

EYES

No matter which position you choose, you will want to rest your hands in a mudra, eyes softly downcast, with your spinal column straight.

If you follow these instructions, you should be in the perfect position to breathe and remain comfortable for the duration of your practice session.

STEP 6: SUCCESSIVE TRIPS

It's time to start walking your cat!

So the first thing I want you to do is sit down. Sounds a bit nutty, and it is, but there's definitely cause.

So you've got your cat harnessed up, you've checked the fit, clipped on the leash, and headed for the door. Your cat has expectations. He's done this before, he knows the routine. But it's time to change things up.

As you step outside, carry your cat somewhere else. Preferably, out to the sidewalk in front of your place. If it's too noisy or there's too much traffic, carry your cat to a different location (or, if necessary, drive it there). Set your cat on the ground and then sit on the ground beside your cat. Put your cat in your lap and talk to him softly.

Continue for five minutes, giving your cat time to take in some of the sights, sounds, and odors before beginning your walk. I know, it looks silly, but it's important that you just don't throw your cat into the deep end. Your cat needs time to decide whether this new place is safe.

If, after five minutes, your cat isn't ready to explore, or is clingy, give him another five minutes. If he's still not ready to move from your lap, that's it for this trip. Take your cat back inside, all the while telling him how proud you are that he faced up to its fears and that tomorrow will be another day.

The next day, try again. And the day after. And the day after that. Until your cat has decided that it's safe, and slowly climbs out of your lap and onto the sidewalk. Some cats will do this the first time out, others may take a few days. It doesn't matter. Each time you take your cat out, he's gaining important information. About the neighborhood. About the perceived dangers and lack thereof. About you.

If your cat climbs out of your lap and walks back toward the house, that's okay. Let him. And call it a day. Once inside, give it a treat, spoil him mercilessly for a few minutes, and then let him hop in the window and watch the world from a safe vantage.

Now, if you have an aerial dog run or a mobile tie-out, it's time to use it. Alternate between your walks and tying your cat out on the aerial dog run or the mobile tie-out. It's really important that you stay outside with your cat when you tie him out to ensure he's safe from neighborhood animals and that he doesn't get tangled in the tie-out. Why is this so important? For one thing, it allows your cat to gather a lot of experiential information in a more secure environment (your backyard or a fenced-in or hedged garden). Second, and equally important, as we mentioned earlier, the aerial dog lead/mobile tie-out teaches your cat that once he comes to the end of its lead, he must change direction to continue on. This is a huge lesson, and if you're consistent, it may mean the difference between having a cat you can lead and one who leads you. I would suggest, in the beginning, keeping him on the lead for 30–45 minutes before going in. On days when you're working in the yard, extend the time as necessary, stopping every so often to pet your cat and remind him what a superstar he is.

Make sure your cat has water and food handy if you plan to stay outside longer than an hour. In the summer, also make sure there's an opportunity for your cat to get out of the sun.

Back to the walking part. You're probably going to want to walk the same corridor for a while, which is understandable. Just throw in a new or novel location every five days or so. Maybe an uncrowded park. Walking trails. Even a shopping district. Got a café with outdoor seating? Definitely worth a try. See if you can get your cat to sit calmly in your lap while you sip your drink.

So how do you actually walk your cat? We've talked about the various types of walking cats, but you won't know for sure what you have initially, so let's assume you have a trotter. At first you may need to do some more backward walking as you coerce your cat with treats and/or his favorite toy. If he gets scared and refuses to move or pulls in the opposite direction, sit down on the sidewalk with your cat and gently talk to him. It doesn't matter what you say, just talk softly and keep a pleasant tone. And then, after a couple minutes, your cat may surprise you and start walking again. If not, pick your cat up, carry him past the current house and when you get to the next one, set him down and begin walking again. Your cat may balk again. Stop, give him time, but remember, don't give in to pulling. Be the aerial dog run! If you must let him sniff a leaf that's just out of reach, move a step in the direction so that the cat doesn't reach the end of his lead and begin to pull—beat your cat to it. If you're not consistent with this, you'll send your cat the wrong message and lose one of the main benefits of using the aerial dog lead/mobile tie-out.

Also, cats love hedges and walls. They love to walk right up beside them. Initially, you'll need to accept this, as what's actually going on is that your cat feels safer. There's one less direction they have to monitor. Don't be surprised if your cat stops when the hedge ends and the driveway begins. A lot of cats will feel totally exposed and out in the open in these cases. If your cat stops at every driveway and opening, simply pick your cat up and carry him past the driveway. Once the hedgerow or walls start again, place your cat on the ground and keep walking. No consoling or baby talk in this case. You want to treat these impasses as if nothing out of the ordinary is going on. Just pick up the cat, walk past the driveway, and place your cat back on the ground.

After a while, start to wait your cat out. Instead of immediately picking him up when the hedgerow stops, wait 20 or 30 seconds. One day, when you least expect it, your cat will slink past the opening. A few dozen walks later, he will walk quickly past the opening. And then, one day, he will walk normally past, his eyes forward, no longer terrified something bad will happen.

Other Animals

Unless Oprah invites me on her show, you're not likely to run into many other people walking their cats, but you will encounter dog walkers. And depending on where you live, it might be a frequent occurrence. When a dog walker approaches, pick up your cat. Even if your cat was raised with dogs or the dog walker states, "my dog loves cats," don't take a chance. Animal interactions can be quite unpredictable, as can animal owners. Better safe than sorry. Even if the dog walker stops to chat, hang on to your cat. If your cat gets antsy and wants down, excuse yourself and walk past the dog walker before putting your cat back down on the ground. Seriously, unless you know the dog walker and your cat knows the dog and they're buddies, well, just don't do it.

While I stated that you're not likely to encounter many cats on leash, you will run into free-roaming cats. In most cases, the free roamer will be very interested, and your cat may return the interest, but the free roamer, not knowing you, is not likely to approach. If it does, again, pick up your cat. In my years of cat walking, though a couple cats have come fairly close, they've always kept a pretty safe distance from my cat. This shouldn't be an issue.

OTHER ANIMALS, PART 2

Other animals, also known as people, are another issue entirely. They're almost never on leash and tend to be pretty bold. While some cats see all people as friends, most don't. Depending on how many people interacted with your cat during early socialization will have an impact on how they deal with strangers. Most cats fear them.

If your cat flattens himself to the ground when a person approaches, or pulls, trying to get away, simply pick your cat up and carry it past the person. Once you're a good ten feet away, put your cat down and continue on your way. Most cats will look back and then hustle a bit, trying to get as much distance from the person as possible. Don't make a fuss. Just lift, carry, place. You don't want your cat to feel like there is a reason for concern. You want your cat to learn that people passing aren't going to bother them, and for some cats, this is the hardest lesson of all. You will see improvement if you're patient and consistent. If you see someone coming toward you, before your cat notices, pick up your cat and pass by. Avoiding the stress altogether can aid in reducing the time it takes for your cat to become comfortable with people. Your cat may never welcome strangers' attention, but it can learn to tolerate it. Remain consistent and vigilant and you'll see improvement.

Then there are kids. Kids often barrel into a cat's space, freaking them out by the sheer impropriety of it all, so again, when you see a kid coming your way, do a preemptive carry and get your cat past the child before it invades the cat's space.

And finally, expect to meet your neighbors. Cat people especially, as you'll find that most people are amazed by a cat on leash and will stop and ask you about it. In the early days, keep your conversations brief if your cat shows signs of anxiety. Explain that your cat is learning this new skill and you have to go. They'll understand and watch bemusedly as you continue on your way.

Using the Outdoor Facilities

Because walking leads to pooing, you'll need to carry a poop bag, just like your dog-walking brethren. I'm sorry to say, you'll no longer have that little bon mot to hold arrogantly over your dog-walking friends' heads. Picking up poop is now part of your future. Get used to it.

Don't get arrogant if your cat doesn't use the outdoor facilities. It's likely a temporary condition. Your cat may be too frightened to put himself in such a vulnerable position, but one day, all that will change and you may find yourself needing poo bags as much as the dog walkers.

If, after a couple months of practice, your cat isn't using the outdoor facilities but immediately does so upon reaching home, you may need to teach your cat that it's okay to go outdoors. If you have a regular path you take, before your walk find a spot that your cat usually sniffs and pour a cup of your cat's litter there. Used litter is best because it has the appropriate smells. Then, as you pass, your cat is likely to notice, stop, smell, and potentially paw at the spot. It may take a few walks, but eventually your cat will get the idea and before you know it, he will be using the outdoor facilities pretty regularly.

You may be thinking you're okay with your cat waiting until he gets home to do its business. I was. But as you become a cat walker and extend and expand your time away from home, your cat will need to get over its fear and use the outdoor facilities. I actually took a kitten on a fairly long walk, and it started crying. I thought I'd tired him out, so picked him up and began carrying him home. Before we made it, the kitten did number 2 in my arms. It wasn't pleasant, so I taught him to use the outdoor facilities using the litter method I just described. After that, any time we were out for more than half an hour, he would dig a hole and do his business.

Signs of Success

Depending on your cat, he may take to walking relatively quickly, but most take some time. Watch his tail. A scared cat's tail will be lowered as it walks through the neighborhood. As his confidence builds, every once in a while his tail will raise, and then, rather quickly, fall again. As the practice continues, you may see it rise more and more frequently, until it's up during the entire walk. I guarantee the first time you see that tail go up, you're going to break into a beauteous smile and you feel proud of your cat, and proud that you've worked so hard to give your cat this, the outdoors. And you'll realize that there's no better gift.

Your cat may also become very loving on your walks and stop to solicit your attention. I have a cat who does this and it reminds me that the work, the love, the caring I've shown my cat is being returned tenfold, and though it was a lot of work, I'd do it again in a minute.

CAT WALKER: LINDA AHRENS

PROFESSIONAL CAT BREEDER, FELINE BEHAVIORIST, EVENT COORDINATOR, AND CAT WALKER

Linda Ahrens has been breeding and showing Oriental Shorthairs for over 20 years. "In every litter, there's one cat that's special," she says, and her cat Zenyatta is one of them. "She loves attention. She's a show cat, and loves being carried to the show ring and getting all that attention."

She also loves walking.

"In 25 years of breeding cats, she's the only cat I ever kept. When I turn off the television she jumps on my shoulder and we go to bed." Their relationship, she explains, is something special. The bond they have is one of both love and trust.

At the time of the interview, Zenyatta was seven years old.

EARLY DAYS

Ahrens began training Zenyatta in earnest when Zenyatta was six months old. Zenyatta was well-suited to leash training. "She is a very outgoing cat. She's not afraid of anything, even putting the harness on her didn't bother her."

TRAINING DAYS

Ahrens was lucky. Fearless cats are somewhat rare, but if you've got one it's much easier to get them to walk on leash than less brave cats. After all, all cats long to be out there, but it's their fear, heightened by the tyranny of the leash, that keeps them from fully embracing the opportunity to go outside.

"It took a while to train her to walk with me. You let them figure it out. I would let her tell me when she was ready to go."

On their outings, she gives Zenyatta a few minutes to do her thing; walking about, sniffing, and eating grass. Then, she would encourage Zenyatta to follow her.

Ahrens explains that with other cats, she's started by letting them get used to the harness. She's taken adults out who've never been out and been successful. "It's about patience. You don't want it to be a bad experience. If they're really afraid, I take them back in."

As for the dash-and-run problem, Ahrens explains: "I never, ever, allow them to walk over the threshold. When I open the door and they come to the door, I stomp my feet and clap my hands loudly to startle them. Zenyatta knows she can't go out on her own. I pick her up and carry her out the door. Always.

It takes a while to get them to follow you like a dog because a cat has a mind of its own. Trying to drag them here or there doesn't work. I don't walk her, she walks me. After a while I can get her attention. I gently say, 'come on, Zenyatta,' and give her a little tug."

FOLLOWING THE LEADER

Zenyatta is both leader and follower. Ahrens lets Zenyatta do her thing first and then, after a few minutes, she coerces her to follow with a verbal cue and a gentle tug on the leash. Most times Zenyatta follows.

"I lead her to areas she'll like, like woodpiles where she can eat spiderwebs!"

While Ahrens often walks Zenyatta in the neighborhood, she's also ventured outside of Zenyatta's home territory.

"I've taken her to the park in Fresno, but steered clear of the dog park. The park is large, so I found a quiet area to walk in. In my experience, Zenyatta is 1 in maybe 500 when it comes to cats. If you get that cat to trust you, that cat will do anything for you. They feed off of your emotions."

Why did she decide to train Zenyatta? "I'd had a dog that had been my traveling companion, so I initially trained Zenyatta for that purpose. But life changes, and as a breeder, I began spending more and more time indoors with my cat litters."

TOOLS OF THE TRADE

Ahrens uses a cloth harness with Zenyatta because every Oriental has a different body shape. "Cloth harnesses wrap around their body and create a secure feeling." As for a leash, she's never used a retractable leash, but considers giving it a try. She currently uses a standard cat leash.

CAT–WALKING TIPS

Ahern says the first thing you must do is get them used to wearing the harness. She suggests you put it on and let them get used to it for five minutes on day one. "To throw a foreign thing around their body is pretty disturbing for a cat. They must feel comfortable in the harness before you move on."

Once they've gotten used to the harness, she suggests you let them lead and set the pace in the beginning. "Always keep in mind that this must be a positive experience, which means absolutely no dragging or pulling. In the beginning, let them lead you.

"When I bring out her harness, she comes running!"

—*Linda Aherns*

ZAZEN: CREATING YOUR SPACE

"If you are depressed, you are living in the past.

"If you are anxious, you are living in the future.

"If you are at peace, you are living in the present."

—*Lao Tzu, ancient Chinese philosopher*

Creating a space, both physical and mental, is important if you're going to create a regular practice. The space should be as free from distractions as possible, and in the early stages, this includes your cat.

Your cat, seeing you calmly seated, will want to investigate. You'll be giving off positive loving energy and your cat will likely climb in your lap. Your cat will probably be giving off his own loving energy and, despite the symbiotic beauty of this, it's too much to navigate for those new to meditation. We'll talk about the possibility of meditating with your cat later, but this really isn't a first-year activity.

Controlling your cat is as simple as closing the door, but what about the other members of your family? Get support from your partner and kids, explaining how important this is to you. If the kids aren't old enough or able to provide you the space you require, consider meditating before they get up and after they go to bed. While some meditation practices warn about meditating too late in the evening (you could fall asleep), you shouldn't be too worried about it. Any meditation is good, no matter what time of day, so don't let that become an excuse.

The nice thing is you don't need very much space to meditate. You don't need any accoutrements either; no candles, incense, etc. In fact, you could make space in a walk-in closet, a basement, or even the laundry room if space is at a premium. You just need a spot that's not too warm or cold, allows a modicum of privacy, and is always available when you need it.

DIRECTING YOUR CAT

We've discussed the three types of cats and only one is relatively easy to coerce into going in the direction you want, and even then, there are days when your cat just won't cooperate. One thing we know about cats is that, while they love us dearly, at their core, they're steadfastly independent. A cat knows what he wants and getting it involves determination and smarts. That's how they survive.

So it's normal, and natural, for your cat to want to go his own way. It's part of being a cat. To get him to follow your lead, it has to be your cat's idea, or, at least he has to believe it's his idea. He should see following you as more desirable than all those delicious (or dangerous) smells and sounds that are assaulting his senses.

If you're still having problems getting your cat to follow your lead, the following tips might help.

- Always allow your cat to root and check out things, unless they're dangerous or too far out of range.
- Never, ever drag your cat. If you do, he won't see following your lead as desirable and will use everything in his power to do the opposite. So instead of pulling, hold your ground. Let your cat pull, but don't pull back. When possible, wait your cat out. If he doesn't move in a reasonable amount of time, pick him up, walk 5–10 feet, and put him down again. After a while, your cat will get tired of the game (after a long while) and decide that going in your direction is more desirable. It will be your cat's choice. Praise your cat and offer it a treat. Then take a couple steps away, make the leash taut, and wait for your cat to join you. When he does, give him another treat. After doing this a few times, reduce the treats to every other time, and then every third time. Always couple treats with a "Good kitty!"

- Treats are a powerful tool, but if your cat is anxious or afraid, it will not be interested in the treats. Keep trying. In time he will take the treat, and you'll know that definite progress has been made.
- If you aren't using an aerial dog lead or mobile tie-out, consider adding them to your practice. This is the best way to teach your cat that, once he comes to the end of its leash, he must change direction.

CAT WALKER: RACHEL LARRIS

POLITICO, FEMINIST, PUBLIC RELATIONS SPECIALIST, AND CAT WALKER

Princess Caroline, a Lynx Point Siamese mix, is Rachel Larris's first cat. After spending a pleasant hour chatting with Larris, I'm certain Princess Caroline won't be her last cat. Being a professional writer as well as a new pet owner, Larris maintains a blog and a diary in which she documented her journey from cat owner to cat walker in exacting detail, providing readers with a peek into her process.

EARLY DAYS

Larris began training Princess Caroline when she was 11 months old. Because Larris was between jobs, she had quite a bit of time to devote to the process and took things slowly, always conscious of Princess Caroline's needs.

Larris told me that she is still in the process of training Princess Caroline, and she didn't feel this was an activity that would ever be "done." Rather, she feels this is something that her cat would continue to improve at over time. She walks her cat mainly in the neighborhood complex, but has taken a couple of trips to a park. "The park trips didn't go well; there was too much stimulation for Princess Caroline in the park."

"I wasn't sure about it when I started training her to walk on a leash, but now I feel it's something anyone can do. It's kind of a magical feeling when you get a predictable response from an animal."

—*Rachel Larris*

WHO LEADS WHO

Princess Caroline likes to eat grass and climb trees on her walks. She's an investigator and does a lot of sniffing and checking out of her surroundings. When they do walk, Larris allows Princess Caroline to set the pace and the direction.

When asked how Princess Caroline responds on windy days, Larris noted a behavioral change. "Today the wind was really strong and she let me know that she was ready to go back in. Windy days are not something she enjoys."

TOOLS OF THE TRADE

She used a dog harness in the past, but now has a more decorative harness that she likes better. Initially, it was too big for

Princess Caroline, but she grew into it. She uses a standard cat leash.

Tip: See her blog...

Zazen: Creating a Regular Practice

The Zen master poured his visitor's teacup full, and then kept pouring.

The visitor watched until he could no longer restrain himself.

"It is overfull. No more will go in!"

"Like this cup," the Zen master said, "you are full of your own opinions and assumptions. How can you learn truth until you first empty your cup?"

—Zen koan

Creating a regular practice that is something you look forward to is one of the most important aspects of meditation. In the beginning, quieting the mind is pretty daunting. Your practice may feel like a chore, something you should do rather than want to do.

In the beginning keep reminding yourself why you're doing this, and tell yourself that there is a finite number of sessions you'll have to endure before you begin to notice the benefits. And the benefits will be life affirming.

Think of your meditation sessions as something you do, like brushing your teeth, because you know it's good for you. Once you've established a routine, it won't take long before you begin to feel refreshed after a meditation session, and it will change from something you do to something you want to do.

If you decide to meditate 15 minutes, twice a day, you'll need a means of knowing when time's up. Some instructors say that you should just look up at the clock from time to time. I found that to be really disruptive, especially on brain noisy days where I felt like the time was dragging. Each time I looked up, the minute hand had barely moved and I had to work to return my attention to my breathing. I quickly gave up on the clock and downloaded a meditation timer app for my phone. It chimes, softly, at the midpoint of my meditation session and then at the end. Having the midpoint chime makes it easier to keep from checking the time. When I hear the midpoint chime, I have a sense of where I am in the meditation and it's easier to return my focus to my breathing. There are quite a few meditation timers and guided meditation programs in your phone's app store, so if you decide to go this route, you will probably find one you like.

If you don't want to use a phone app, you could use a PC app, an egg timer, or even the timer on the stove. Anything that works for you and keeps you from worrying about how long you have left will make it easier to maintain your practice.

Finally, if you find yourself fidgeting and having a difficult time making it until the timer goes off, shorten your meditation time. If, in the beginning, all you feel capable of doing is five minutes, that's how many minutes you should meditate. Over time, as your meditation muscles firm up, you'll be able to slowly increase the length of your meditations. Be patient with yourself; even five minutes is valuable. The length of your sitting is not as important as keeping on a regular meditation schedule.

PART III
ENLIGHTENMENT

This section celebrates your success and talks about what it means to have a leash-trained cat and a calm mind.

REGULAR WALKS

In time, your cat will come to look forward to his walks and his outdoor time on an aerial lead or mobile tie-out. Just as you need to carve out a regular time for your meditation, you need to do so for your cat walks, too.

How often should you walk your cat?

Every day, if possible, but for most people, it's not, especially in the early days, when going for a walk is something of a production. Don't overcommit; that's a sure way to fall off the wagon. Instead, give it a month with the intent of taking your cat out whenever possible. Keep track of the times you actually take your cat out. If you notice a pattern, like you tend to take your cat for a walk on Wednesdays after work and Sundays after brunch, choose those days and times as your scheduled regular walks. Got time on a Thursday? Go for it, just don't decide that since you went on Thursday you can skip your regularly scheduled post-brunch Sunday walk. Extra walks are just that, not an excuse to alter your schedule.

Your cat needs to see that these walks are regular, or else they'll forever be at the door, trying to dash out whenever you open it. If your cat understands that another trip is just around the corner, your cat will be more relaxed about his walks and less likely to try to slip out the door. If, despite being fairly consistent with your schedule your cat still does a mad dash for the door every time you open it, consider increasing the number of days per week or the duration. Also, combine yard work with cat time and secure your cat using an aerial dog lead or a mobile tie-out while you're weeding, puttering in the garden, or watering the lawn. Just make sure Kitty is out of the sprinkler's range!

Night Walks

In addition to varying the places you walk, you should also vary the times. If your cat finds his daytime walks daunting, give a night walk a shot. You may find that your cat comes to life once the sun goes down. If nights don't work for you, try predawn. Even cats who have begun to enjoy their regular daytime walks may get a serious thrill out of walking after the sun has set or before it's risen. Cats, being crepuscular, meaning they're most active at dusk or dawn, love going outside when there's no sun. The only downside is that your cat is likely to see a lot more stuff than you do, so remember to be the leash and don't give in when your cat pulls. I've given this its own section, because it's a really important step in getting your cat comfortable with walking on leash. Alternating between dusk or dawn walks and daytime walks may help your cat get over his fears more quickly. Also, because the sounds of the neighborhood are at their quietest, your cat will likely be less anxious.

My cat Puma, who is still afraid of people when out walking, is positively electrified by night walks. Every ten feet or so he stops, turns and looks behind, and then turns back and continues on his way. The first time we went out on a night walk, I thought the constant looking back was due to nervousness, but quickly realized it wasn't. I was watching a predator at home, fully aware and excited by his surroundings. The night was his time to shine, and I watched, amazed and happy, as he took in the sights and the sounds of the night that were hidden from me. When we arrived back home, his tail was held high and he was happier than I'd seen him in a long time. I gave him some treats and told him he was a good boy. And then, instead of heading for the porch, he turned back toward the neighborhood, eager to go exploring some more.

Depending on where you live, summers can be brutally hot, and though your cat may want to go out, the pavement may be too hot for your cat's paws. At those times, dusk and dawn may be the only real options, so this is another reason for varying the times you walk your cat.

Cat Walker: Sara Fabel

Tattoo Artist, Dad Joke Enthusiast, and Cat Walker

Sara Fabel and Dawn, her ebony ticked Oriental Shorthair, have been going on walks for a couple of years now. Oriental Shorthairs are known to be talkers, and Dawn lives up to the breed trait. "We talk to each other a lot and she follows me from room to room. When she's in another room she'll call for me and I'll call back, and then she comes to see me."

Fabel's next challenge: "I want to get Dawn a safety jacket so I can try taking her kayaking with me."

Dawn was three years old at the time of the interview.

Training Days

Sara began to train Dawn when she was about six months old. "It took about 10 days for her to get used to the harness, and then another month to get her used to our trips to the pet store."

She continues to get better at walking on a leash, but progress has slowed. "In the beginning, change was quick, but

once she'd reached a certain point things slowed down."

"I'm happy to have Dawn as my best friend."

—*Sara Fabel*

When ruminating on Dawn's training, Fabel says: "Early in her training I took her on a weeklong RV trip and she made a lot of progress."

In addition to the RV trip and trips to the pet store, they've also gone camping. When at home, they regularly walk through the neighborhood. They live in a gated community that sounds like a cat walker's dream. "It has an aviary surrounded by benches and dogs are not allowed in the community. Everyone has a pond, so there are lots of things for Dawn to explore on our walks."

As for how Dawn deals with the weather, Fabel says: "She won't go out if it's raining or it's windy. She won't even go out on the porch."

FOLLOWING THE LEADER

Fabel and Dawn have worked out a pretty wonderful compromise. When they leave home, Fabel leads. On the way back, Dawn leads. "When she's had enough, she's very determined. Sometimes on the way home I have to ask her to slow down. She loves to jog, so I jog along beside her."

TOOLS OF THE TRADE

Fabel uses walking jackets with Dawn. "They provide a lot of coverage. Straps are uncomfortable and you have to make them really tight. Dawn wouldn't walk with the straps; we went through four different harnesses until we found one that she found comfortable."

Fabel uses a retractable leash with Dawn. "The traditional leashes touched her, and made a sound when it dragged, which bothered her. I switched to a retractable one."

Cat-Walking Tip

Fabel says to take it slow and make the training something enjoyable. With Dawn, she only gave her treats and played with her when she had the harness on. Then she began to play with her on the patio, associating her time outside with playtime. It's important, Fabel says, to make it something your cat will look forward to.

Exposure to New Places and Experiences

I've already mentioned the importance of wandering outside your regular neighborhood on a regular basis. The reason is twofold. If you don't, or rarely do so, your cat will habituate on his regular neighborhood, but in a specific rather than general manner. The first time you take your cat to a new location for his walk, it will definitely feel like your cat has regressed to the level of fear he experienced on his very first outing. The truth is, its fear level won't be nearly as extreme.

Your cat will engage in collecting experiential data again, which will make your cat extra cautious. Over time, as you expose it to more and more places, the experiential data will begin to overlap and your cat will no longer have to collect as much data before making a decision that it's safe.

Need to return the electric drill you borrowed from your brother-in-law? Perfect. Harness up your cat and take him with you. When you get to your brother-in-law's house, take your cat for a short walk in his neighborhood. This helps the cat get used to riding in the car, too. Too many cat owners only take their cats for a ride when they're going to the veterinarian's office. While there are exceptions to every rule, most cats don't enjoy going to see the vet. If the only time you take your cat for a car trip it gets prodded, injected, and manhandled, he will see the car in a very negative light, and getting your cat into the car could be a chore.

If you're training a young kitten, once it has all its shots, take him everywhere. Going to pick up dinner at the drive-through? Harness up your kitten and take him along for the ride. Need to get more kibble? Take your kitten to the pet store. Hanging out at an outdoor café? Harness up your kitten and work on getting him to sit calmly in your lap while you sip and read. But don't forget to take some of your kitten's favorite treats with you.

What about older kittens and cats? Is it too late for them? Absolutely not! The only difference, really, is that it may take many more trips to get your older cat to accept change. Remember, much of what your cat fears is the tyranny of the leash—his inability to run for the hills if he feels like he's in danger. Be cognizant of this, be loving, and above all, be patient. Your cat is a smart animal, and though all the stimulation will initially be overwhelming, you are enriching and enhancing his life.

Try to take your cat to a new location every fifth walk or so. This doesn't have to be anything elaborate; while a new neighborhood doesn't seem all that different to you, for a cat, this is huge. Try to find locations that include things that your cat likes. Is there a community garden full of butterflies? A café with an outdoor patio? A duck pond? Finding places you think your cat might enjoy will make the experience more special for your cat and shorten the time it takes to get your cat to accept new places.

Zazen: Meditating with Your Cat

"Our way is to practice one step at a time, one breath at a time, with no gaining idea."
—*Shunryu Suzuki, Soto Zen monk and teacher*

If the cat is the ultimate meditator, why not invite it to join you in your practice? Whether or not you buy into my assertion, you may find that when meditating, your cat will want to join you.

While I feel meditating with your cat is a worthy goal, it's not for everyone. In the early days of your practice, when you're still working to maintain your focus, it's not recommended. Find a spot where you can close yourself off from your cats so you can meditate undisturbed.

Once you've created a regular practice and outside distractions no longer destroy your calm, it may be time to open the door and let your cat in. When I'm meditating, one or more of my cats will usually come into the room and climb into my lap. I don't seek them out or call for them, they come of their own accord. After settling in, they often begin grooming themselves and purring.

I continue to concentrate on my breathing unless the purring is regular and loud. In those cases, I'll gently shift my attention from my breathing to the sound of the purr and then shift back to my breathing when the purr becomes uneven or ceases altogether. I also acknowledge the weight and the warmth of the cat, but mainly I stay focused on my own breathing and the cat's purr. I may stroke the cat a few times, but that generally pulls me from my focus so I try to avoid it. While I don't know if this will work for you, it works for me, and concentrating on the cat I love so much, while sharing time with him, makes the time fly by and enhances my ability to transmit loving kindness during my meditation.

I often wonder if my cat is meditating too, or just dozing. It certainly seems like sleep, as my cats often spend the first five minutes or so grooming themselves before settling down. Then, when they've settled in, I'm generally deep within my own session and no longer really aware of their state. I'm still aware of the warm weight and the gentle rumble of the purr, but these sensations are fleeting as I focus inward.

While I can't say if they're meditating too, they're definitely responding to my stillness and my calm. They seem to be enjoying the loving energy I'm giving off and I believe that a sharing of sorts is taking place. I imagine they're responding to the fact that for a small period of time, I'm exhibiting a cat-like calm that they effortlessly slip in and out of all day long.

Cat Walker: Scot Fortino

Photographer, Photographer's Assistant, Dispatcher and Driver for a Medical Pharmacy, Ranch Caretaker, and Cat Walker

Scot Fortino lives in West Covina, California with his Egyptian Mau, Romulus. Fortino is one of the lucky ones; Romulus came from the breeder already partially leash trained. He and Romulus enjoy walks that Fortino describes as "dog-like." Because Romulus is deaf, he doesn't hear most sounds and so noises have never been a problem for them. Romulus also enjoys people and dogs, so there aren't many things that faze Romulus on their walks. Starting early, Fortino feels, is the secret to ending up with a cat who takes to the leash readily. In addition to regular walks, they'll sometimes just hang out in the yard.

At the time of the interview, Romulus was 13 years old.

Early Days

Fortino got Romulus from a breeder when Romulus was 14 weeks old. Romulus was already used to wearing a harness when he arrived. "I didn't take him out until he had completed his shots," Fortinio explains. "It was almost natural for him. I just started to walk and he started following me. I'd tug on his leash and he would walk with me. Cats hate harnesses, so if you start out early you will have more luck."

The more they ventured out, the better Romulus got.

"He loves going to Petco. He likes to ride on my shoulder as we make our way through the store. His favorite spot is the cat aisle."

—*Scot Fortino*

FOLLOWING THE LEADER

Fortino and Romulus go for walks two to three times a week. On their walks, Fortino is the leader and Romulus generally walks behind. They often walk through the neighborhood; up the block and back. Romulus keeps pace with Fortino, who is able to maintain his normal walking speed. Like most cats, Romulus takes time to nibble on grass along the way.

They also make occasional trips outside their neighborhood and one of Romulus's favorite outings is Petco.

He's also well-acclimated to the car and will lay in the back window and watch the world roll by. When asked how Romulus responds to windy days or days when the weather isn't California beautiful, Fortino explained they only go out on nice days.

Tools of the Trade

Fortino uses a harness with clips when he suits up Romulus, and uses a standard leash.

Cat–Walking Tips

When asked what advice he had for prospective cat walkers, Fortino provided the following:

When you get the harness, be patient, and let him wear it in the house before you take him out. When you put on the harness, make sure it's secure but not too tight. You should be able to get two or three fingers between cat and harness. A lot of cats become fearful or immobile when you put something on them, so get them used to the harness before venturing outdoors. After you get used to each other, and your cat gets used to the harness, you can take him outside. If you're training a kitten, it may take to it right away, but if you're training an older cat it will take a little time. Be patient.

ZAZEN: THE PROMISE OF ENLIGHTENMENT

"To the mind that is still, the whole universe surrenders."
—Lao Tzu, ancient Chinese philosopher

In Zen Buddhism, the ultimate goal is enlightenment; an awakening, a state of being where the answers to all your questions are within your grasp and the true nature of your true self is revealed. A lot of people practice Zen in hopes of gaining enlightenment. I'm not reaching for that lofty goal; I'm satisfied with the enhanced calm, reduced stress, and the greater sense of contentment and well-being my practice affords. The nice thing about meditation is that many of the little changes you experience over time are permanent. Once you've learned to let go, the ability doesn't really go away with disuse. There have been periods in my life where regular meditation wasn't possible for one reason or another. When I returned to my practice, it was there, waiting for me. The skills I'd gained were there, in full force, and I was able to slip back into my routine in an amazingly short time. When I think about it, and look back on the periods when I wasn't meditating, I realize that my ability to let go and emotionally detach from my discursive thoughts was still there. The person I was before was gone for good.

I don't want to downplay enlightenment. If I ever gain it, I surely won't turn my back on it. But that's not why I embarked on this journey. To my mind, enlightenment is just an accumulation of what you gain daily from your regular practice. Enlightenment is like a bank; you start out with a few pennies, and, with each meditation, you drop another coin in that bank until, one day, you wake up and realize it's full.

Namaste.

NOTES

NOTES

NOTES

NOTES

NOTES

NOTES

NOTES

NOTES

NOTES

NOTES

Notes

NOTES

NOTES

NOTES

TOILET TRAIN YOUR CAT, PLAIN AND SIMPLE
An Incredible, Practical, Foolproof Guide to #1 and #2

CLIFFORD BROOKS
$12.99 | 5½ x 8 IN. | 128 PAGES
PAPERBACK ISBN: 978-1-5107-0725-2 | EBOOK ISBN: 978-1-5107-0726-9

Get rid of the litter box!

Teach your cat the coolest trick in the book—literally! *Toilet Train Your Cat, Plain and Simple* is your guide to getting rid of the litter box and learning to share the throne with Queen Mittens. Author Clifford Brooks has successfully trained all of his cats to use the toilet and wants to share his tips with you. This book will help you do just that with features such as:

* Step-by-step instructions on gradually training your cat to use a toilet
* Helpful tips from an experienced cat owner
* Clever, sophisticated illustrations

Unlike other kitty-training manuals with far-fetched promises, this guide takes a realistic approach with tips on best practices and suggestions for useful items to purchase or have on hand throughout the training process. Brooks's humorous tone makes this guide as fun to read as its end results are rewarding. Cat owners everywhere should read this book. Just imagine: you'll never scoop poop again.